The
Gospel of Thomas:

Where Science Meets Spirituality

Also By Lee and Steven Hager

The Beginning of Fearlessness:
Quantum Prodigal Son

Religious or Spiritual:
How the Difference Can Affect
Your Happiness

Lee and Steven Hager

The Gospel of Thomas:
Where Science Meets Spirituality

Oroborus Books

The Gospel of Thomas:
Where Science Meets Spirituality

Copyright © 2011 by Lee and Steven Hager

All rights reserved. Printed in the United States of America. No part of this book may be used, reproduced or transmitted in any manner whatsoever including electronic, mechanical, photocopying, recording, by any information storage and retieval system, scanning, uploading or distribution via the Internet without written permission by the publisher.

Published by **Oroborus Books**

The Beginning of Fearlessness/Oroborus Books website:

www.thebeginningoffearlessness.com

ISBN 13: 0978526163
ISBN 10: 978-0-9785261-6-0
LCCN: 2011936756

This book is dedicated to everyone who feels certain there must be something greater than what the eye sees, the ear hears or the hand touches.

A man should look for what is, not what he thinks should be.—Albert Einstein

The attitude of faith is to let go and become open to truth, whatever it might turn out to be.—Alan Watts

Without going outside, you may know the whole world. without looking through the window, you may know the ways of heaven.—Lao Tzu

Contents

Introduction
12

Chapter One
A Very Different Jesus
18

Chapter Two
What Is Gnosis?
26

Chapter Three
Quantum Physics Primer
40

Chapter Four
The First Few Puzzle Pieces
64

Chapter Five
Liberation
80

Chapter Six
What Is the Kingdom?
96

Chapter Seven
Here, There, Everywhere
110

Chapter Eight
Beings of Light
122

Chapter Nine
Two Masters
132

Chapter Ten
What No Eye Has Seen
152

Afterword
188

Index
193

The Gospel of Thomas:
Where Science Meets Spirituality

Introduction

What is a spiritual master? Why do they seem so different, so 'other-worldly?' Where does their wisdom come from? When confronted with a master, we try to come to logical conclusions. Since they seem so very different, we quickly assume they must have come from outside our universe or been specially chosen by a supernatural power and given extraordinary gifts. But in this case, logic would have failed us.

Ask any master and they will tell you they are an ordinary person who has had a direct, personal experience of the Divine. Moreover, they will encourage you to have the same experience. This is always shocking information, and few choose to accept it. We've been conditioned to believe that we need someone else to save us. Having our own direct experience of the Divine seems impossible, frightening or even arrogant. So instead of following in the master's footsteps, we filter the master's message through our own world view, dilute it and make it more palatable. In the process we lose the real message and try to limp along on the crumbs. We hope the master will become our savior and carry us on his/her back. But masters share their experience to show us the door is open, not to carry us through it. Their words are meant to inspire our own exploration and personal experience of the Divine, not serve as a substitute for it.

The direct personal experience opens the sage's eyes and they see the universe as it actually is, not as they had been conditioned to see it. Jesus was one of these masters. Unfortunately, unless a follower also has a direct experience, they cannot fully understand what the master is saying, and they are left to interpret the master's words through their own perception.

Sadly, we have no accurate eye-witness accounts of Jesus' life and teachings. Instead, we have the words of many of his followers, some who understood what he was saying and many who didn't. Some of the information is contained in the gnostic gospels, some in the New Testament. Neither of these sources is more accurate than the other or more authentic. Since that's the case, how can we follow Jesus' footsteps?

Cutting edge research in quantum physics presents a compelling picture of the structure and operation of the universe that's startlingly different from the universe we thought we lived in. Although this information appears to be catapulting us into a new era of understanding, it has been available for centuries. Spiritual masters found that when they experienced the Divine, they also saw the universe as it actually is. As their misperceptions were replaced with truth, they understood everything in a new way. When we look at Jesus' teachings in light of quantum research, it becomes obvious that Jesus saw and understood the universe as it actually is. Since it was impossible for him to speak in terms of quantum physics, he tailored his message to his audience as best he could.

As we read accounts of Jesus' life and teachings, two very different pictures of Jesus emerge. One image corresponds with quantum research; the other cannot be reconciled with our quantum universe. One set of information is presented by those who emulated Jesus and experienced the Divine for themselves. The other set reflects the apocalyptic views prevalent in Jesus' day, including a passionate desire for a savior that would release the Jews from their Roman oppressors and restore their theocratic nation. When Jesus died, his apocalyptic followers were left with two choices. They could look at Jesus' message from a different perspective, or they could manipulate Jesus' story and teachings to fit their new circumstances.

We also have a choice to make. Are we willing to take a 'quantum' approach to Jesus' teachings? Do we want to find out what Jesus' had to say about our universe? Or will we cling to an outdated view that cannot be reconciled with scientific research? Einstein recognized, "Science without religion is lame. Religion without science is blind." Saint Thomas Aquinas agreed saying, "Revelation comes in two books—the Bible and Nature…a mistake about nature results in a mistake about God."

We've discovered that the synergy of science and spirituality has the power to transform your life. We invite you to join us in exploring Jesus' parables and sayings from a quantum perspective. But like Jesus, it is not our intention to give you more words to follow, but to offer a reason for you to want to experience the Divine for yourself.

Introduction

Chapter One

A Very Different Jesus

The *Gospel of Thomas* contains only 114 of Jesus' sayings, but its powerful message has rocked conventional understanding of who Jesus was and what he taught. In *Thomas*, Jesus is not a savior, a messiah or a Christ. He does not die for anyone's sins, and resurrection is not even mentioned. He is not considered the only-begotten Son of God, God incarnate or even a master over his followers. If he's not portrayed in any of the roles that are customarily assigned to him, what part does he play?

The *Gospel of Thomas* quotes Jesus as saying, "I am not your master...He who will drink from my mouth will become as I am; I myself will become he...When you come to know yourselves...you will realize that it is you who are the sons of the living Father." Jesus is a master, but like all true masters, he knows that he is master over no one but himself. He offers what he has experienced, but only as a jumping off point for his followers' own spiritual quest.

The gnostic *Gospel of Truth* confirms Jesus' position as a wisdom teacher saying, "He became a guide, a person of rest who was busy in places of instruction. He came forward and spoke the word as a teacher."

Later in the *Gospel of Truth* the writer adds, "He appeared, informing them of the Father, the illimitable, and he inspired them with what is in the mind…For a doctor rushes to where there is sickness, since that is the doctor's wish." It's not surprising to see Jesus portrayed as a healer, but in the gnostic gospels the healing work Jesus undertakes is not the miraculous sort so prevalent in the New Testament. And it's not a temporary physical healing, but a permanent healing of the misperceptions that keep humanity locked in misery.

Thomas opens by telling us, "Whoever finds the interpretation of these sayings will not experience death." Here Jesus focuses on healing the mind because he's discovered the mind is the place where problems originate, and also where they're healed. Instead of having faith in the person of Jesus, salvation was found by unraveling and understanding his message, by exchanging misperception for truth. This gnostic message confirms Jesus' words in the New Testament at John 8:32, "And you will know the truth, and the truth will set you free."

In the New Testament, sin is considered an inescapable, inherited deficiency that causes us to fall short of perfection and condemns all humanity to death because, "...sin came into the world through one man and death through sin, and so death spread to all men because all men sinned." (Romans 5:12) Hebrews 9:22 tells us "without the shedding of blood, no forgiveness takes place." In this case, God can only overlook original sin by shedding precious blood.

But in *Thomas*, Jesus says, "What sin have I committed or how have I been undone?" Jesus wasn't claiming that he was exempt from sin through Divine birth, but that sin was not at all what his followers had been taught to believe it was. In the *Gospel of Mary*, Peter asked Jesus, "What is the sin of the world?" Jesus replied, "There is no such thing as a sin" and explained, "This is why you get sick and die; because you love what deceives you." In fact, Jesus' gnostic followers believed in original goodness.

The gnostic focus on healing the mind becomes more understandable when we realize that Jesus equated 'sin' with ignorance. This form of ignorance wasn't related to a lack of education. It's better understood as willful forgetfulness of our Source and our true identity as beloved children of the Divine. Ignorance was considered a mistake that could be corrected at the level of the mind, not a defect that required a bloody sacrifice as atonement. In fact, ignorance is not connected to any form of Divine anger or punishment. Instead, we must each accept the consequences of our own choice to remain blind to truth.

As you read, you'll discover that early Christians were not the tightly knit group we've been taught to believe they were. In fact, the argument over who and what Jesus really was raged on within the institutionalized church for several centuries. During that time, Jesus' persona ranged from human to adopted son of God to demi-god (half God, half human) to only-begotten Son of God to God incarnate and finally to triune Godhead. The debate between Jesus' humanity vs. divinity was finally decided by the Roman Emperor, Theodosius, who declared that "all true Christians" must accept the trinity doctrine or be branded as heretics and punished. Once Theodosius made his decree, it was all but forgotten that a sizable group of Christians, both gnostic and orthodox, had believed whole-heartedly in Jesus' humanity. Why should this matter to us?

If Jesus was either the only-begotten Son of God, God incarnate or part of a Trinitarian Godhead, we must agree that humans misused the God-given gift of free will and are reaping the consequences: sin and death. We must agree that without Divine intercession, we are beyond salvation. In that case there is little we can do except believe in Jesus' shed blood and obey. But, if Jesus was a human wisdom teacher that discovered we had estranged ourselves from the Divine but could be reunited in love, we've found an example we can all follow. This path requires self-responsibility, but it is a path of joy that liberates us from any feeling of fear, hopelessness or condemnation.

Although it's now thought that the *Gospel of Thomas* is probably as old as the earliest New Testament gospels, no authentic eye witness accounts of Jesus' life and teachings exist. No early Christian writings are any more valid, authentic or trustworthy than any others. No one 'owns' Jesus or has the right to dictate where truth can be found or which interpretation of his story is correct.

Regardless of which gospel accounts we read, orthodox or gnostic, it's imperative to remember that we're reading someone else's opinion, not historic fact. No matter how pure they felt their motives were, each and every writer had an agenda they were promoting. It happens now, it happened then. Regardless, every Christian sincerely interested in Jesus' teachings owes it to themselves to find out what early gnostic Christians had to say. Decide for yourself what *you* think. Listen to your own heart; let it tell you what resonates with truth. The *Gospel of Thomas* is about a living Jesus, one who is present now and ready to interact with you.

A Very Different Jesus

Chapter Two

What Is Gnosis?

Since the gnostic gospels were discovered in an earthenware jar at Nag Hammadi, Egypt in 1945, gnosis has become a popular subject. And like all popular subjects, conflicting information about gnosis and the gnostic gospels has quickly accumulated. Currently, gnosis is associated with everything from magical to metaphysical ideas, astral travel to out of body experiences. But gnosis is actually a concept that has held far-reaching significance for spiritual seekers for centuries.

Gnosis is an ancient Greek word that actually means 'knowing' or 'knowledge,' but this is not the kind of knowledge that we attain through intellectual pursuits. This form of knowing is experiential; it comes through having a direct, personal experience. Riding a bicycle is experiential. Someone else can tell you how to ride, you can read instructions or watch others ride, but you will 'know' how to ride only by having the experience. When you have acquired this 'knowing,' you will understand bicycle riding, but it will be impossible for you to transfer your 'knowing' to anyone else. You can describe the balance and momentum needed to keep the bicycle moving, but your words won't be any more effective than those who tried to teach you.

The word gnosis can be applied to anything that requires our direct, personal experience to understand. However, in the purest sense, it means a direct, personal experience of Divine Presence. Most of us have been conditioned to believe that we must approach the Divine through a mediator like Jesus. But Jesus, along with every other spiritual master, attests to the fact that everyone has the right and the ability to meet the Divine directly. This concept is known as the perennial philosophy, and gnosis plays an essential part in it. The Perennial Philosophy is a golden thread of spiritual thought that has run through virtually all cultures, eras and areas of the globe for the last twenty-five centuries. Although it contains much more, Aldous Huxley's book *The Perennial Philosophy* boils down the main concepts of the philosophy to a few basic thoughts:

There is a Divine Ground that permeates the universe.

The world we think we see is a temporary projection that originates from that Divine Ground.

A change of consciousness is required to become aware of, and experience, the Divine.

Everyone has the ability to experience the Divine.

Experiencing the Divine is life's highest purpose.

Simply put, *life-giving intelligence permeates everything in existence. This intelligence wants to be known and can be known.* Gnosis is the means we all can use to reach that knowing. As we go through the *Gospel of Thomas*, we'll discuss many of Jesus' cryptic sayings that point to, and explain, gnosis.

Although gnosis is associated with a 'change' in consciousness, this change is not associated with paranormal activity nor does it require that a seeker enter an altered state of consciousness. It simply means that we begin thinking from the mind rather than the brain. This may sound odd, but scientists have recently discovered that the brain and the mind are not the same thing. The brain is an exceptionally sophisticated computer-like organ and receiving unit, but the mind is not part of the brain. Science now understands that the mind is a field of conscious energy that permeates and connects everything in existence. Many physicists are beginning to think of this universal consciousness as the One Mind of God.

In the gnostic writing *Dialogue of the Savior*, the teacher Silvanus explained the importance of accessing this universal mind. He wrote, "Bring in your guide and your teacher. The mind is the guide…live according to your mind…acquire strength, for the mind is strong...enlighten your mind…light the lamp within you." As Silvanus pointed out, gnosis takes place when we let go of the brain's preconceived notions and access the One Mind we share with the Divine. The mind has no limitations, and is our best possible guide.

The Difference between Gnosis and Gnosticism

The word Gnosticism is out of sync with the definition of gnosis. When we add the suffix 'ism' to a word, it then describes a distinctive doctrine, theory, system, or practice such as Catholicism, Judaism or Buddhism. Although organizations have been formed that label themselves gnostic, the individual experience central to gnosis makes it impossible to organize, let alone institutionalize. Gnosis can't be experienced through another person, a sacred book or a belief system. Although you can easily find those who claim otherwise, the word itself tells us there can be no dogma, practices, rituals, systems, rules or doctrines involved in gnosis.

If we do choose to use the word Gnosticism, it is more accurately described as a dynamic spiritual approach, a direct, personal, intuitive process. As author James Hillman pointed out, "Intuition is clear, quick, and full. Like a revelation, it comes all at once and fast." It comes to us through the heart as well as the mind and is accompanied by a feeling of peace and clarity.

What Are the Gnostic Gospels?

When we hear the word gospel, we usually think of a holy book or sacred text. Would you be surprised to know that the Greek word for gospel, *euaggelion*, originally described a style of writing we currently refer to as 'self-help?' For early Christians, gospels weren't histories or accurate eye-witness accounts, they were writings aimed at personal transformation. Like current self-help books, the writers offered their own viewpoints and opinions. Gospels were also persuasive writings used to convince others to follow a certain path or join a certain group of believers. In a way, we could think of them more as propaganda than inspired narrative.

In Jesus' day, only a small minority knew how to read and even fewer could write since writing was a skill practiced by scribes. Jesus' earliest followers were among the uneducated masses, so they passed their stories around orally. Written gospels started circulating among more educated Greek speaking Christian converts about 25-30 years after Jesus died. The names of Jesus' disciples were attached to most gospels to give them a more authoritative voice, but it's extremely doubtful that anyone who had actually met Jesus wrote them, or even contributed to them. During the first two centuries after Jesus' death, his story went through many transformations, and was used to support several divergent agendas.

Early Christians had hundreds of gospels to choose from. During the first three centuries after Jesus' death, Christianity was extremely diverse. Each gospel that circulated offered a different slant of Jesus' life and teachings. When you take a close look at the Bible gospels, you'll see that none of them tell the same story about Jesus, and in each he has a very different persona. This happened primarily because each of the gospels was written for a specific audience. The writer of Matthew directed his message to Jews alone. The author of Mark had a mixed audience of Jews and gentiles, while Luke's author wrote specifically for a non-Jewish audience. John was written for an audience that wanted to avoid any connection to Judaism and instead attach itself to the Roman Empire.

Since it was impossible to know exactly what Jesus did, said or meant, none of these groups could prove their viewpoint was correct. And conversely, no one could prove they were incorrect. As the stories circulated, people began to align themselves with the stories they believed were true. The 'Peter group' institutionalized their particular beliefs and organized a clergy class to dispense them. This group was eventually supported by the Roman Empire and named itself the orthodox (straight thinking) catholic (universal) church. With the Emperor of Rome backing them, the church made it their business to annihilate any person or group who disagreed with their teachings and policies. Their agenda was so successful, it was only suspected among Bible scholars that early Christians held diverse views. One of the clues was the denunciations made against opposing groups that they regularly found in orthodox Christian literature.

When gospel accounts that described a very different Jesus began to slowly surface, scholars realized there had never been consensus among early Christians. But the independent nature of gnostic Christians contributed to their own demise. Although they passed their writings around, they didn't turn them into sacred texts or dogma. They met informally in each other's homes, but they had no clergy class and were too loosely organized to be considered a church. Early on, gnostic followers of Jesus had been in the majority, but their opposition to organization and literalism made them a special enemy of the organized church. Once the church had destroyed them and their writings, it wasn't long before people forgot they had even existed.

It's important to note that gnosis takes as many forms as Christianity. Many writings that are considered gnostic are only very loosely associated with Christianity and many are pagan. Some groups considered Gnostic were closely associated with ancient 'mystery schools,' that did feel gnosis was a step-by-step process. Their writings are often filled with arcane language that can barely be deciphered. This was done to keep the general reader from understanding the information until they were initiated into higher and higher levels of the belief system. However, there are several gnostic texts that are clearly associated with early Christianity and are as fresh and valuable today as the day they were written. The *Gospel of Thomas* falls into this category. However, when we approach even the most straightforward of the gnostic writings, we find that they're presented in parables and symbols. Why?

Symbolic Language

Gnostic writings were meant to be interactive. The reader did not accept them as irrefutable, inspired or sacred truth, but was expected to search his or her own heart to discover the meaning the Divine was giving them personally. Jesus was a gifted teacher, but unlike other speakers who tell interesting stories, he filled his parables and sayings with symbols. His use of symbolic language is obvious in both the New Testament and gnostic gospels, but many listeners failed to understand this and took his words at face value. But Jesus' gnostic followers understood that he spoke in parables so those who wanted to be spiritually awake would have to extend themselves to discover the deeper meaning. We can listen to the words of a great teacher, but to have any real impact; those words must go past the brain and reach the heart and mind.

Symbolic language is often disregarded as primitive or childlike, but that's far from true. Symbols use pictures, metaphors and analogies that are common to the human experience but allow us to connect with a higher plane of thought. Like love, symbols are something people of all languages, nationalities and time periods can understand. Symbols use concepts we identify with to open our minds to something we don't yet understand. Symbolic language allowed Jesus to craft a message that would continue to resonate down to our day and beyond.

Many of Jesus' early followers confused symbols with signs and misunderstood what he was saying. Signs are something we take literally. When Jesus said that he came "not to bring peace but a sword," many of his followers saw the word sword as a sign of literal weapons and warfare. Those who understood the word symbolically realized that Jesus' words were not meant to console, but would cut through their illusions like a sharp instrument.

If we take Jesus' parables and sayings at face value, we'll learn something. If we're willing to go deeper and search our heart for the symbolic meaning, we'll learn far more. If we make the message our own by using it as inspiration for our own experience of the Divine, it will transform us. Although we'll be discussing the meaning behind the symbols, it's up to you to contemplate the meaning and use it as a basis for your own inner exploration. To make the message your own, follow Jesus into the experience of gnosis. Looking back at the words of Silvanus in the *Dialogue of the Savior*, it's evident that each of us must be responsible for our own spiritual awakening, ". . .bring in

your guide and **your** teacher...Live according to **your mind**...Enlighten **your mind**...**Light the lamp within you**." [bold ours]

The Gnostic/Scientific Connection

Most religions are based on a dualistic belief system. This means that they see the universe as a collection of separate forms. They also believe in a God that's separate from creation and resides outside it. When spiritual seekers throughout the ages have *experienced* the Divine, they've seen past the illusion of separate forms and understood that the universe is one interconnected whole that's permeated by the Divine. It's this direct experience that's allowed spiritual masters like Jesus to say, "I shall give you what no eye has seen, what no ear has heard, what no hand has touched, what has not arisen in the human heart."

One of the most interesting facets of many of the gnostic gospels is their correlation to recent scientific discoveries in the field of quantum physics. This may seem odd, but can be easily explained. When we experience the Creator, the creation is also revealed. Unlike religious dogma, science poses no threat to gnosis, and in fact enhances it.

To get the most from this book, you may wish to read *The Beginning of Fearlessness: Quantum Prodigal Son* first. It offers an in depth look at Jesus' parable of the prodigal son, Jesus' gnostic and New Testament teachings, and the quantum physics that support his words. If you've already read the book you may wish to skip the next chapter, or read it as a refresher. If you haven't read *Quantum Prodigal Son*, the next chapter contains a condensed summary of the quantum principles and background material that will assist you in understanding the *Gospel of Thomas*.

Chapter Three

Quantum Physics Primer

While the discovery of the gnostic gospels was shaking up the foundation of Christian beliefs, quantum physics was rocking the scientific community with unexpected discoveries that have brought into question everything we know about our world. Physics is the branch of science that studies energy and matter and their interactions. Classical or 'Newtonian' physics explains how the visible universe operates. It studies phenomena such as velocity, momentum, movement and gravity and explains the 'laws' or parameters they work within. Quantum means 'amount' in Latin, the word 'quanta' describes the small increments, or parcels, energy can be divided into at the subatomic level.

Quantum physics is still the study of energy, matter and their interactions, but applies to the universe at the invisible, subatomic level. Physicists had assumed the physical laws that governed the visible world would also govern the invisible, but they were shocked to realize that what is unseen operates in an extremely different way than what is seen. On the surface the universe appears to be made up of smaller and smaller separate parts, like building blocks or cogs in a machine. Scientists assumed the parts worked together, but still remained separate. When they took apart the pieces and reassembled them in different ways, they believed they had proven the point. And they felt certain a high percentage of these universal 'building blocks' were inanimate, devoid of life.

But as scientists divided these 'building blocks' into subatomic particles, they were shocked to discover a sea of interconnected energy where no separation or form existed. They realized the universe could no longer be described as a multitude of separate parts, but must be understood as one interrelated, cohesive whole. In fact, they found that the parts, like cells in a body, had no meaning outside the whole. Even more surprising, they discovered even the tiniest subatomic particles were alive and conscious. In essence, the universe itself can be seen as one cohesive, vitally alive, consciousness.

Since classical physics had conditioned scientists to believe most energy and matter was unconscious, they saw themselves as objective observers who collected and measured the data that resulted from their experiments. But everything changed when experimenters discovered that they became conscious participants in quantum experiments. No matter how determined they were to remain detached observers, their involvement was unavoidable. Why? Quantum particles exist in a state of potential and have no set or stable state until they're influenced by consciousness. Since scientists couldn't extract themselves from the consciousness that permeated the universe, their thoughts influenced the outcome of their experiments. Physicists realized this interaction was possible only because *all* energy and all matter is conscious. As a result, many physicists began to feel that we live in an intelligent universe.

The Illusion of Separation

Many Eastern philosophies have long contained the central theme of conscious oneness echoed by quantum physics. Over three thousand years ago, the writer of the Brihadaranyaka Upanishad recognized the conscious unity that exists beneath the illusion of separate forms. That ancient writer stated, "As a lump of salt thrown in water dissolves and cannot be taken out again . . . the separate self dissolves in the sea of pure consciousness, infinite and immortal. Separateness arises from identifying the Self with the body, which is made up of the elements; when this physical identification dissolves, there can be no more separate self." In this scenario, the creator does not exist outside creation, but creator and creation exist as one unified whole.

Although we see separate forms in the material world, science is now discovering that separation is indeed an illusion created by the brain and senses. Many eminent neurophysiologists now agree that the brain is an amazing computer and information retrieval system, but the 'mind' is a field of consciousness that cannot be contained in the brain. But the brain and body are necessary tools we need to make sense of our world.

As unbelievable as it sounds, unless consciousness is observing matter, matter appears as energy. Unless someone is observing it, the tree outside your house exists as an energy pattern. It takes your sensory input filtered through your brain to create the illusion of the material object we've agreed to call a tree. The combination of brain and senses construct the sight, taste, smell, texture or sound that convinces us an object is real. This means that the 'visible' portion of the universe is more aptly described as a virtual reality that's dependent on perception to exist.

Since your body and brain are matter too, they only appear as matter when consciousness observes them! *To be aware of your body, consciousness must exist outside of it.* If this were not the case, it would be impossible for you to distinguish your body from the seething energy field that makes up the quantum universe. If your consciousness is not part of the body then you're not the body. If you're not the body, who are you? Where is your reality, the *real* you?

Our Holographic Universe

Physicist David Bohm used the hologram as a model to explain how the visible and invisible portions of the universe operate. If you've ever seen a hologram, you know that it's a 3D image that appears to float in space. The image appears very real, but it's actually no more than a projection, a virtual reality. When we look at regular photographic, movie or slide film it's easy to see an image of the picture that was taken, but that's not the case with holographic film. Instead, the image is unrecognizable and appears to have no relationship with the image it produces. That because the image is spread over the surface of the film in a series of intersecting patterns, like ripples that spread out and intersect when raindrops hit a pond. Regardless, the "real" part of a hologram is the film, not the projected image. Bohm saw our universe in the same way. He described the material portion of the universe as a holographic image; it seems real, but it's a virtual reality. The quantum level of the universe is like the holographic film; it appears to be nothing more than a sea of energy, but it's real. Bohm realized the quantum level is the seat of consciousness and the source of all energy and potential. The material universe is like a holographic image that's projected from the quantum level.

In truth, we are not the bodies that we project; we are the mind that exists at the quantum level and does the projecting. Our material bodies are part of the quantum soup of All That Is, but they are not our reality. It would be more accurate to think of our bodies as the players that represent us in a video game or an actor that plays our part in a movie. Surprisingly, gnostic Christians were well aware of this phenomenon and called the world an illusion, a dream, nightmare or a drunken stupor. It may seem odd that these ancient people were so astute since they had no access to the research we take for granted today, but we must remember that they had something even more powerful than any sophisticated scientific equipment: gnosis. When they experienced the Divine, they bypassed the limited brain and accessed the one consciousness we all share, the very mind of the Divine. Gnosis allowed them to understand the material and quantum portions of the universe as they actually are.

The gnostic *Gospel of Truth* says the visible universe is, "like a dream in the night." We can wake from our dream of virtual reality anytime we choose, and when we do we will, ". . . see nothing, because the dreams are nothing." Similarly, the beautiful gnostic narrative poem, *The Hymn of the Pearl*, tells the symbolic story of a prince of the spirit realms who journeys to a far country of matter and form. The prince falls asleep, forgetting his true spiritual identity, and is rescued by waking up and remembering who he is. In the *Gospel of Thomas* Jesus likened our virtual reality to inebriation when he said, "I found them all drunk, and I did not find any of them thirsty. My soul ached for the children of humanity because they are blind in their hearts and do not see, for they came into the world empty, and they also seek to depart from the world empty." They were so intoxicated by the world, they had no thirst for the truth that Jesus offered.

One Life, One Mind

We can no longer claim that anything in the cosmos lacks consciousness; it's only the level of intelligence or awareness that differs. We can no longer make a division between the animate and inanimate since everything in existence shares the spark of life. Nor can we claim that anything but oneness exists. What is this oneness that we call universe? Most scientists are either not ready, or are unwilling, to call it God. But several quantum physicists and astrophysicists have recently come to that conclusion, and they are willing to say so. And from a spiritual perspective, those who have experienced the Divine have long proclaimed that the universe and the Divine are synonymous.

Many religions continue to teach that God exists outside creation, but gnostic writers agreed that the Divine permeates and supports and sustains everything in existence. The gnostic teacher Monoimus expanded on this point by adding, "Look for Him [God] by taking yourself as the starting point. Learn who it is within you. . . you will find Him in yourself." For Gnostics, God's kingdom is not a place or a thing; it is "an immediate and continuing spiritual reality," a state of conscious being we can experience at any time. The *Aitareya Upanishad*, written nearly 3,000 years ago, described how God (the Self) brought the universe into existence:

> *Before the world was created, the Self*
>
> *Alone existed; nothing whatever stirred.*
>
> *Then the Self thought: "Let me create the world."*
>
> *He brought forth all the worlds out of himself.*

The *Chandogya Upanishad* elaborates on this thought, explaining why everything in the universe is part of one indivisible whole:

In the beginning was only Being.

One without a second.

Out of himself he brought forth the cosmos

And entered into everything in it.

There is nothing that does not come from him.

Of everything he is the inmost Self.

He is the truth; the Self supreme.

You are that. . .you are that.

As the sages recognized, everything in existence came out of Source and therefore *is* Source. This isn't difficult to grasp when we apply the same pattern to procreation that takes place in the material world; the offspring of humans and animals are all made from, and nourished by, the material of their parents. Likewise, the seed can only come from the material of the parent plant.

Birth of the Universe

Evolutionary scientists tell us that the universe came out of nothing, by accident, and continues to exist through an incredible series of lucky breaks. They claim life is the result of a random mixture of dead chemicals that suddenly came to life. On the other hand, quantum physics tells us that all energy is life and life is energy. They've discovered that it takes consciousness directed at energy to transform energy into matter. So, within the universe we find the consciousness and energy needed to spark the Big Bang, keep the universe finely tuned and cover the earth with life forms. If we decide this matrix of consciousness and energy potential is the Divine, we naturally want to know how the Divine brought the material portion of the universe out of Self.

It would be impossible for us to say exactly what happened at the inception of the universe, but spiritual masters inform us everything began with a creative thought. Scientists add that our entire universe came into existence from an infinitesimally tiny amount of 'source material' somewhere between one ounce and a billionth the size of a subatomic proton! It's estimated the visible universe was 'born' nearly 14 billion years ago during a colossal explosion known as the Big Bang. If you've seen the devastation caused by the violent eruption of a volcano, it seems impossible to believe anything of value could ever come out of such a cataclysmic explosion. The name Big Bang implies that the beginning of our universe was just such a catastrophe, but the evidence tells quite a different story.

In 1983 Alan Guth first suggested the theory of inflation, which is now supported by research. Guth proposed that when the universe was less than a trillionth of a trillionth of a second old, it experienced an extremely brief, hyper-explosive growth spurt. The first explosive expansion was incredibly fast. Steven Hawking said that this would be similar to taking a small coin and expanding it to ten times the size of the Milky Way in far less than a second! If the initial dab of source material hadn't expanded at a rate that's faster than the speed of light, the heat produced in a slower explosion would probably still be cooling.

When an explosion takes place on earth, there is no design to it and nothing constructive results. But the Big Bang caused the universe to expand in an extremely uniform manner that served as a foundation for all that was to come. However, the expansion still contained just the right amount of irregularities needed to bring stars, planets and galaxies into existence. These irregularities had greater density, which caused gravity to draw matter together in those places. Without this delicate balance of uniformity and irregularity, galaxies that can support life couldn't exist.

This source material has been expanding ever since the Big Bang and scientists have calculated the expansion is speeding up. If that's the case, why doesn't the universe fly apart? When we look at the night sky, we see what appears to be 'empty space' between the stars and planets, but it's far from empty. Two-thirds of the universe is a seething ocean of quantum energy that far outweighs matter. Scientists have been unable to explain why this seemingly impossible disparity exists, but they do feel that the heavyweight energy opposes gravity and is responsible for keeping the universe stable as it expands. This 'cosmological constant' is very finely tuned. Without it, the universe would have either imploded or been ripped apart.

We can dismiss this information as interesting scientific trivia, or we can see it as nature's testimony that everything in existence came from one Source and remains one interconnected whole. We can think of life as a mindless accident, or we can recognize the intelligence of All That Is. We can insist that some of the universe is alive but much of it isn't, or we can recognize the life force and consciousness that permeates all things. We can believe that the universe arose out of nothing and will return to nothing, or we can look at the fine tuning that keeps everything necessary to life in delicate balance and conclude that the Divine and the universe are synonymous.

Why Create?

But why would Source create? Many religions believe that God created to provide himself with obedient worshipers. Eastern traditions often explain that the material world was created because Source desired self-knowledge and wanted to gain it by experiencing through creation. Either of these views turns humans into little more than pawns in a cosmic game played by an all-powerful despotic madman who enjoys human misery.

Spiritual masters have another answer. Every master who has ever had a direct experience of the Divine reports that "God is love," with the emphasis on *is*. They're not talking about an emotion that can be given and taken away; they mean love is the state of Divine Being. The ancient creation hymn *Nasadiya Sukta,* makes the point that love is the foundation of the universe, "In the beginning Love arose, which was the primal germ cell of the mind." The Gnostic writer Valentinus also describes love as the ultimate motivation for creation:

Since the Father was creative, it seemed good to him to create and produce what was most beautiful and most perfect to himself. For he was all love and love is not love if there is nothing to be loved.

The 13th century Sufi mystical poet, Rumi, also recognized the same motivation when he said, "Without Love, nothing in the world would have life." But Ultimate Reality's desire to love could never be satisfied by robotic clones that lack free will. Obviously, love can only be appreciated, exchanged and expressed between beings that can choose for themselves and exercise free will. Although many scientists are 'determinists' who believe everything we do is predetermined by genetics or past occurrences, quantum physics has demonstrated that we live in a universe of free will and choice. Since the universe depends on consciousness to act on energy potential; nothing happens without choice. It was choice that brought the material universe into existence, and it's the choices we make each day that continue projecting our world of seemingly separate forms.

Duality, Separation, Scarcity and the Battle for Specialness

Many religions teach that God gave his human creations free will, but then punished them when they exercised it. A one choice option can hardly be called free will, and it has nothing to do with love. If that's the case, why do we appear to exist in a material world of separate forms? Why is there so little love and so much suffering? What we see in this world appears to be the opposite of everything quantum physics has taught us about the oneness of the universe. How can separation and oneness exist at the same time?

The key to this mystery lies in the fact that the material world exists only as a projection of consciousness. Nothing that happens in our world, no matter how horrific it appears to be, can actually damage anything that's real. As conscious creations of the Divine, we've been given the ability and free will to 'imagine' anything we want and project it as a harmless material virtual reality. The gnostic gospels make it clear that what we're experiencing is no more real than a dream. But like a dream, we're convinced it's real while it's happening.

Jesus' parable of the prodigal son described the choice made by conscious beings to discard the equality of oneness and seek specialness. To do that, the material world had to be based on a foundation of 'polarized duality.' Specialness can't exist if everything is special; to have specialness, 'not special' must also exist. Duality provides the needed contrast because it consists of two irreducible modes that oppose one another such as hot/cold, high/low, right/wrong, good/bad. In polarized duality, we cling to the pole we believe is positive and reject the negative. Everyone wants the positive but that desire, of course, is impossible. Duality, like the lottery, creates very few winners at the expense of millions of losers.

Competition and scarcity are the inevitable result of polarized duality. Since everyone wants the things that make us special in this world, from the day we're born we join a constant battle to obtain them. Instead of thinking in terms of cooperation, this thought system convinces us that we must take from others if we are going to have what we believe is necessary to our specialness. If we find it impossible to be special by gaining what the world prizes, we try negative forms of specialness. Regardless, we're all in a constant quest to set ourselves apart somehow and procure what we think will make us happy. But duality is merely a mental construct; it's not the only way to perceive our world. Unfortunately, dualistic thinking is so ingrained; we rarely recognize its existence. And sadly, we've become so enmeshed in duality and separation, we've forgotten that we can return to oneness anytime we wish.

If you haven't read *The Beginning of Fearlessness: Quantum Prodigal Son*, it will also be helpful to become familiar with the definitions of these often used terms:

One Mind:

Consciousness that is the foundation of the universe and permeates everything in existence.

The One Mind we share with the Divine.

Our 'higher' or 'true mind.'

False Mind:

In order to project our dualistic virtual reality, some changes had to take place in the One Mind we share with All That Is. To fully experience the illusion of separation, a portion of our mind had to be partitioned off to contain the dualistic thoughts that conflict with oneness. When we think with the One Mind, it's as if we are living in a magnificent sunlit mansion. When we think with the closed off portion we call the false mind, it's as if we've gone into a tiny, dank, windowless room in the cellar and locked ourselves in. The mansion still exists, but if we stay in the cellar long enough, we forget it's there.

Many fail to recognize the existence of the false mind and confuse it with the ego. The ego is a brain-based sense of self; it's the belief that we are an individual human being. Since the ego defends and protects the body and our vision of self, it's a tool that's necessary to navigate this world. The ego can present its own difficulties, but it's still not the false mind. Instead, the false mind is conflicted consciousness that keeps us locked in virtual reality. It helps us forget our true identity and convinces us we *are* the body and the personality that the world has constructed for us.

Since the false mind is a closed off portion of the One Mind, it doesn't connect itself to a specific personality or body, but continues from lifetime to lifetime. The false mind is not an 'evil' separate entity. It's a thought system that was born out of our desire for separation and specialness and it can only continue to exist within the confines of that dualistic thought system. When we choose to return to oneness and think from the One Mind, we strip away our beliefs in separation and specialness. But this is done lovingly; fighting the false mind only makes it stronger. When we stop feeding the false mind with the thoughts that support it, it's like a plant without sun, it shrivels and disappears into the soil it came from.

self:

The body and personality we project in virtual reality. We use the terms false self and false mind interchangeably. (The 's' will always be in lower case.)

Self:

The unique conscious being that you truly are in quantum reality. (The 'S' will always be in upper case.)

The Self is not a life force or a soul that inhabits the body. This is the Divine you that shares your existence with Source. The terms Self, true Self, true mind and One Mind will be used interchangeably. The term Self is also used at times, especially in the Upanishads, to refer to the Divine.

As we progress through the parables and sayings in this book, these basic principles should become clearer. As you read, please keep in mind that no one knows what Jesus actually said. When we quote Jesus' words we realize the source may or may not be accurate. What we've looked for is the general flavor of the words and teachings and for their consistency with the understanding of a spiritual master who has experienced the Divine.

As quantum understanding increases, many belief systems will be challenged. Much of institutionalized Christianity will not be able to withstand the challenge, but gnosis, based on our innate ability to directly access the Mind of God at the quantum level, will. Jesus understood what got us here, and in the *Gospel of Thomas* he shares a message that can help us return to our reality in oneness. It's our desire that by the end of this book, you will be ready to follow Jesus' example and experience the Divine yourself.

Quantum Physics Primer

Chapter Four

The First Few Puzzle Pieces

Of all the writings discovered at Nag Hammadi, the *Gospel of Thomas* is undoubtedly the most accessible and well-known. The book feels familiar in many ways because several of the sayings have parallels in the New Testament, but the direction taken by the *Gospel of Thomas* is decidedly different. Some scholars hesitate to label the book gnostic because it resembles the New Testament gospels more than many of the more radical writings that are labeled gnostic. But if we define gnosis as the direct, personal experience of the Divine, it's evident that Jesus' understanding came through gnosis.

Sayings Gospels

The way the *Gospel of Thomas* is formatted tells us a great deal. *Thomas* is strictly a collection of wisdom sayings, parables and stories with virtually no narrative information. There are no references to dates, places or events, and no stories that tell the reader about Jesus' life or try to convince the reader that he's extraordinary. Unlike the New Testament gospels that concentrate on the person of Jesus and point to him being the messiah, *Thomas* ignores the person of Jesus and focuses on his message. In this sense, *Thomas* is very similar to the lost *Sayings Gospel of Q*.

The New Testament gospels Matthew and Luke both had used the gospel of Mark as source material, but scholars found another source hidden within them. Although it's extremely unlikely the writers of Matthew and Luke knew each other, these two gospels shared an additional 4,500 words that were so similar, it could not be coincidence. This source material predated the New Testament gospels, but no manuscripts could be found. Scholars have continued to authenticate this material since 1838, and have compiled it into a sayings gospel called *Q*, which stands for the German word *quelle* or 'source.' Scholars feel that 'sayings gospels' like *Q* and *Thomas* were the original style of writing that circulated among early Christians. Why is that important?

The New Testament gospels are written in a persuasive, narrative style that was designed to convince readers that they should accept

Jesus as their messiah and savior. The narrative style allows the writer to direct the reader's attention and move them toward the conclusions the writer wants them to reach. On the other hand, the series of sayings presented in *Thomas* and *Q* requires the reader to take responsibility and tease their own meaning out of Jesus' words. Instead of seeing the change from sayings to narrative as a more sophisticated understanding of Jesus, we would argue that it was actually used to shift the focus away from the message and on to the messenger.

This shift highlights the wide diversity among Jesus' early followers. While many viewed Jesus from the gnostic perspective, others saw him from an 'apocalyptic' viewpoint. These followers were among the many groups of Jews who were ardently looking for a warrior king who would release them from their Roman oppressors. The apocalyptic view had its roots in hundreds of years of Jewish oppression. The Jews reasoned that God had justly punished them when they failed to keep the law, but they couldn't understand the oppression they suffered when they diligently kept the law.

The Apocalyptic/Messianic View

As the Bible book of Job illustrates, the Jews came to believe that the universe was locked in a cosmic struggle between good and evil. Satan, one of God's renegade sons, had supposedly challenged God by claiming that humans only served God for what they could get out of it. In turn, God claimed humans were obedient out of love. God gave Satan free reign to cause the suffering that would be used to test human loyalty. The Jews believed that when God was finally satisfied with the results of this test, he would send a warrior who would destroy their enemies and establish a literal government on earth.

Jesus' apocalyptic followers believed Jesus was that warrior chosen by God, but their hopes were dashed when he was crucified by the very oppressors they assumed he would vanquish. Instead of trying to understand his message in a different way, they tried to make his message fit their view. They decided if Jesus was not going save them while he was in the flesh, he would return in heavenly glory during their lifetime. When that didn't happen, they decided the test was going to continue, but when Jesus finally returned, he would destroy God's enemies on a worldwide basis. The Jewish apocalyptic belief that began as the desire for a Jewish theocracy became a Christian belief that predicts a decisive victory for God at the battle of Armageddon. They still claim this battle will be led by Jesus, now known as Michael.

Who Is Jesus?

When we look at the wide chasm between gnostic and orthodox views, it's no wonder that the message found in the New Testament often feels extremely conflicted. At one moment Jesus is portrayed as a tender and merciful teacher, at the next, a wrathful and judgmental warrior. In one breath he admonishes his followers to love their enemies, the next moment he tells them they can't follow him unless they hate their own families. Thomas Jefferson was so disturbed by this disparity; he felt he had no choice but to create his own version of the New Testament.

When we consider how ambiguous the Jesus story eventually became, it's little wonder it's been used to inspire the loftiest behavior and rationalize some of the most hurtful. This problem is easier to manage when we understand that each writer saw Jesus through their own perception and wrote about him with their own agenda. Because Jesus' apocalyptic followers didn't understand his gnostic teachings, many of them were included in the New Testament gospels and were either ignored or were given an apocalyptic interpretation. This leaves readers with the sometimes difficult job of deciphering which is which. When we read the *Gospel of Thomas*, the reader must let go of the messianic ideas presented in the Bible to get the full flavor of its meaning.

The Gnostic Jesus

Among the Nag Hammadi writings were two versions of *Thomas*, one in Greek, the other in Coptic, a language derived from ancient Egyptian. The Greek version contains only 39 verses to the Coptic's 114. We'll be quoting from both, but all quotes will be from the Coptic version unless otherwise indicated. At times there are small variations in wording which will be noted. *Thomas* opens with a phase that will prove to be of great significance for every reader:

> *These are the hidden sayings that the living Jesus spoke and Judas Thomas the Twin recorded. And he said, "Whoever*

discovers the interpretation of these sayings will not taste death."

As you can see, the immediate emphasis is on the teachings, not the teacher. Instead of telling the reader to put faith in Jesus as savior, readers are instructed to take personal responsibility and seek out the meaning of Jesus' words so they can save themselves. As indicated earlier, *Thomas* makes no mention of either Jesus' death or a resurrection. Although Jesus had already been crucified when the book was written, the writer speaks of Jesus in the present tense calling him, "the living Jesus." This writing style is carried out throughout the gospel and infers that Jesus' flesh may have died, but he is alive and still available to his followers. When Jesus said that anyone who understands his message will not taste death, he wanted his listeners to understand life in an entirely new way.

We tend to look at life in the material world as linear; we're born, we grow old, we die. But when we look at the regenerative pattern that's in continual operation in the universe, we can see that the universe is cyclical. As science has discovered, matter can appear as energy, and energy as matter, but the sum total of the whole never changes, and nothing 'dies' in the process. An immortal yet changing universe makes sense when we know the universe and the Divine are synonymous. How can we understand this? When we think of the death of the body, we've been taught to see this as the end of the personality associated with it. The body does return to energy and the personality does disappear, but the immortal consciousness that projected them remains untouched by this change. When we understand this, Jesus' promise takes on new meaning.

Gnostics viewed Jesus as an immortal consciousness who, like the rest of us, had projected a human body in order to experience separation and specialness. They did feel that there was one important difference between them: Jesus 'woke up' from the dream of specialness and was once again aware of his true nature. They were drawn to Jesus not because they thought he was special, but they recognized that he had done something they wanted to do. They understood that they would never wake up by turning him into an object of worship or by mimicking him. After all, we cannot create a cause by repeating an effect. But they did know that he had sayings that could stimulate their connection with the One Mind.

To Christians who have been taught that Jesus was either the literal only begotten Son of God, or part of a Trinitarian Godhead, these statements might seem quite shocking. But gnostic writers, along with the authors of *Thomas, Q* and the New Testament gospel of Mark all speak of Jesus in fully human terms. As we mentioned in the Introduction, an extremely heated argument raged for centuries after Jesus' death within the church as Christians tried to decide whether Jesus was human or divine. Once Theodosius declared that "all true Christians" must profess belief in the trinity, Roman forces assisted the institutionalized church in their agenda to destroy anyone who disagreed with them. As often is the case, it's good to remember that might does not make right.

We bring this up again because the question of Jesus' nature holds weighty implications for all of us, which are made clear in *Thomas*. If we examine the New Testament gospels in the order in which they were written (Mark, Matthew, Luke, John), a steady change in Jesus' persona becomes apparent. He begins as a human wisdom teacher or prophet, and then becomes a human adopted by God. Next he is changed into a demi god (½ human, ½ god) by followers who were formerly pagan, and then is made a God in his own right in the New Testament gospel of John. He is finally made equal to the God of the Old Testament by the trinity doctrine.

Remember that it was not only gnostic Christians that said Jesus was human, but a significant percentage of the institutionalized church agreed well into the 4th century. But during the time Jesus' persona was being questioned and changed, church leaders came to the conclusion that without a divine intercessor, sinful humans were lost and beyond salvation. The opposing view maintained that the human Jesus was an example all of us could follow and eventually each of us could have a direct, personal relationship with the Divine, just as Jesus did. Unless you feel certain the church has been authorized to make these decisions for you, these two views leave you with an important choice.

Although the New Testament is focused on identifying Jesus as the messiah, in *Thomas*, the term is not used. When Jesus' followers brought up their messianic/apocalyptic concerns by asking "When will the kingdom come?" Jesus gently chides them by reminding them that God's kingdom "is spread out upon the earth, and people do not see it." When they ask "When will the new world come?" He tells them, "What you look for has come, but you do not know it." When they keep insisting "Twenty-four prophets have spoken in Israel, and they all spoke of you," he answers, "You have disregarded the living one who is in your presence and have spoken of the dead." They were so set in their apocalyptic world view, they were determined to listen to the words of dead prophets rather than a living Jesus who was telling them he was not the messiah and the kingdom was not the literal government they thought it would be. Since they were unable to let go of their apocalyptic views, their brains filtered everything Jesus said and did through their preconceived notions.

Jesus' 'Twin'

In one instance in *Thomas,* Jesus did call himself "son of man." In the New Testament this term is often capitalized to demonstrate that Jesus was different from his followers, set apart because of a special kinship with God.

But scholars say the term is correctly translated as "child of humanity," which carries the same meaning as our saying we're part of the human race. The name given to the *Gospel of Thomas* also testifies to Jesus' humanity. Modern readers might miss the reason the name Thomas was used, but early Christians would understand its significance. Several gnostic writings are attributed to Thomas because the name meant twin. In the gnostic *Book of Thomas* (not the same text as the *Gospel of Thomas*) Jesus says:

> *While you are still in the world, listen to me and I shall reveal to you what you have thought about in your heart. Since it is said that you are my twin and true friend, examine yourself and understand who you are, how you exist, and how you will come to be. Since you are to be called my brother, it is not fitting for you to be ignorant of yourself.*

This passage has caused some Christians to believe Jesus was addressing a literal twin brother, but that doesn't take into account that Jesus puts brotherhood in the future and appears to make it contingent on some accomplishment. The name Thomas does mean twin, and Jesus' gnostic followers used it for that particular reason. However, they did not have a physical brotherhood in mind. Instead, they were suggesting that each follower who comes to an understanding of Jesus' words becomes his twin and partakes of the same connection with the Divine. In *Thomas*, Jesus is pictured as a spiritual brother and guide who considers his teaching successful when his students attain, or exceed, his own level of awareness. This point is made clear when Jesus says:

> *Whoever drinks from my mouth will become like me; I myself shall become that person, and the hidden things will be revealed to that person.*

> *I am not your teacher. Because you have drunk, you have become intoxicated from the bubbling spring that I have tended.*

These sayings make it obvious that everyone has the opportunity to drink the same waters that quenched Jesus' spiritual thirst. Although he tended the bubbling springs, he was not the master of it, and no one was obliged to go through him to get to it. Jesus' sayings offered living water that allows us to become his twin in understanding. But he also emphasizes the fact that no one, including him, can drink the water for us. When we quench our spiritual thirst by contemplating the words of Jesus, we're taking responsibility for our own spiritual awakening, not relying on a savior. Like water, Jesus' words were meant to be ingested, to become part of our being, to become our own.

The First Few Puzzle Pieces

Chapter Five

Liberation

Since Jesus' followers lived in a legalistic religious system that controlled their every thought and action, many of them were understandably looking for a master or leader who would continue to think for them. As a result, they asked Jesus for rules. In the New Testament, Jesus often responded by acting with authority, instructing them and giving them new and different guidelines to follow. But the New Testament also reveals a Jesus who rejected rules and told his followers that the entire law could be dropped if they would learn to love unconditionally. It's Jesus' message of unconditional love that set him apart as one who had experienced the Divine. In a society that thought in terms of discrimination, judgment, justice and revenge, Jesus continually pointed to love as the answer that could free them from every perceived problem.

Jesus' role in *Thomas* is distinctly that of liberator. When his followers questioned him on a point of law asking, "Is circumcision useful or not?" Jesus' sarcastic reply, "If it were useful, children's fathers would produce them already circumcised from their mothers" demonstrated his contempt for anything that was superfluous to love. He wanted to make sure his followers understood the difference between making the prison of the law more comfortable versus escaping from it. To get them on track for liberation he added, "Rather, the true circumcision in spirit has become valuable in every respect." The law had led the Jews to believe ritual, worship, obedience and sacrifice were necessary to gain God's approval, but Jesus was telling them they already had an unbreakable connection to the Divine. Instead of worrying about how the body was behaving, he encouraged them to free themselves of the false self through a 'circumcision' that would cut away anything extraneous to the true Self.

Jesus' rebuff didn't appear to reach their hearts since they also asked, "Do you want us to fast? How should we pray? Should we give to charity? What diet should we observe?" Instead of becoming irritated, Jesus answered, "Do not lie, and do not do what you hate." The rules imposed by their religion allowed very little space for either self-examination or self-determination, yet that's what Jesus was asking of them. Since no one else knows what's in our heart, this 'non-rule' served several purposes. It helped Jesus' followers let go of the legalistic restrictions that encouraged judgment and condemnation of both themselves and others. And even more importantly, it encouraged them to start looking inward and begin examining their own motivations. Like all his other sayings, it was a jumping off point for them to begin understanding they could bypass the religious system and its cadre of priests and rituals in favor of a direct, personal connection with the Divine.

In a society where thinking for one's self was unacceptable, Jesus' approach had to be shocking. It's no wonder that many early followers could not let go of the legalism of the Jewish religion and drug it with them into Christianity. Since many contemporary Christians still feel tied to rules and moral codes, Jesus' encouragement that we examine our own motivation is still fresh and relevant.

Seeking and Finding

The opening words of *Thomas* calls Jesus' teachings "hidden sayings," but not for the reason you might think. The New Testament gospels tell us that Jesus selected a group of twelve men to be his closest companions. These men received visions and secret information held back from others. In *Thomas,* Jesus had companions, but he didn't single out a few to receive special knowledge. In fact, he reassured all his followers, "Know what is before your face and what is hidden from you will be disclosed to you. For there is nothing hidden that will not become apparent." Jesus was actually introducing his followers to information that was 'hiding' in plain sight. They all had equal access to it, but they would have to put some effort into removing the veils that obscured their vision and kept them from seeing it. How would they do this? How can we?

Since we have access to a glut of information and nearly unlimited opportunities for education, many assume that spiritual seeking is an intellectual pursuit, and that is often how we go about trying to understand God. But it's highly unlikely that any of Jesus' earliest followers knew how to read or write and they had very minimal access to education outside of religion. Jesus was certainly not directing his followers to go to established religious leaders for answers since he said, "The Pharisees and the scholars have taken the keys of knowledge and have hidden them. They have not entered, nor have they allowed those who want to enter to do so."

Instead of finding God through education or religion, Jesus offered his listeners something far greater when he said, "I shall give you what no eye has seen, what no ear has heard, what no hand has touched, what has not arisen in the human heart." Obviously, Jesus was offering something that can't be found in the material world. Although many religions view death as the only means of coming into contact with the 'other worldly,' Jesus was thinking of direct contact with the Divine through the One Mind. Accessing Source is not difficult or outside the ability of any of us, but it does take a willingness to see things that fall outside the thought system that supports this world. Jesus regularly made use of a specific teaching tool that can help us dissolve the veils that obscure our connection with the Divine.

The New Testament gospel of Matthew informs us, "All this Jesus said to the crowds in parables; indeed he said nothing to them without a parable" (13:34). Parables and wisdom sayings were meant to engage the listener at a far deeper level than an interesting story or a pithy proverb. As we discussed earlier, the symbolic language Jesus used can reach the listener on several levels. If we take Jesus' parables at face value, we can get some benefit, but we'll miss his deeper message. But it takes a desire to understand and a willingness to plunge into the unknown if we're going to tease out the meaning. That's because symbols encourage us to stop looking for second-hand information that exists outside us, and go inward to commune directly with the One Mind.

The false mind relies on perception for all its learning. As a result, it must hoard and control the second-hand information it accumulates. To break down the barriers of perception that keep us from accessing the One Mind, we must sidestep this stockpile of second-hand information. As we sort the valuable from the valueless, and let go of preconceived notions, attachments, aversions and social conditioning, the veils that have blinded us fall away. We begin to see the body and personality as a useful vehicle for navigating the world, but understand they are not who we are. Many spiritual masters speak of this as "letting go of the self to find the Self." To help his listeners realize that spiritual awakening is an ongoing process and not anything that happens overnight, Jesus said, "Let one who seeks not stop seeking until one finds."

Fasting From the World

Spiritual masters through the ages have agreed that to 'know' the Divine, we must experience the Divine, but like so many religions, Judaism taught the people to fear God. Since the Jews had a large clergy class that served as intermediaries and made sacrifices on their behalf, the idea of connecting directly with the Mind of God must have felt overwhelming. Nonetheless, Jesus' followers could see that he was showing them as well as telling them, this was not only possible, it was liberating. Still, it's no wonder that many of them clung to the messianic views they were familiar with rather than take the risk and responsibility of experiencing the Divine themselves. For the courageous few willing to experience the wonders Jesus had promised, he explained a necessary first step, "If you do not fast from the world, you will not find God's kingdom."

Jesus' followers were used to literal fasting, so how would they "fast from the world?" Again, Jesus was asking his followers to switch their thinking from the actions of the body to what was happening in their mind and heart. Our first thought might be that Jesus was telling them to renounce their possessions or go into seclusion and live an ascetic life. This is often what people do when they seek God, but that's not what Jesus meant. Food was regularly used as a symbol for spiritual sustenance. In the New Testament, Jesus compared bread to spiritual nourishment from God when he said, "Man shall not live by bread alone, but by every word that proceeds from the mouth of God." (Matthew 4:4) The false self must also be nourished to survive, and its 'food' is made up of the dualistic thought system that allows us to project our illusion of separation.

The false mind thrives on any thought or feeling that supports separation and the drive for specialness. When we start looking at the world's thought system, it doesn't take long to figure out that separation and specialness are its very foundation. Even when we believe we have the very best of intentions towards others, we are still part of this thought process. We are constantly in competition with others for the things we think we need, and we often get what we want at the expense of someone else. Just buying a cheap T-shirt may mean the people who produced it must live well below the poverty level. We're not telling you to buy or not buy, only making the point so that you are aware of the fact that as long as we project the world created by the false mind, it's impossible for us to live without hurting others. But when the false self is deprived of the food it depends on for life, it dissolves back into the One Mind. It's like coming out of the dank, dark basement and realizing we do actually live in a sun-filled mansion.

Self-awareness vs. self-improvement

In the light, we clearly see the true Self the false self has been hiding. Jesus was alluding to this when he said, "When you know yourselves then you will be known, and you will understand that you are children of the living Father. But if you do not know yourselves, then you dwell in poverty, and you are poverty." Currently it's popular to believe that we 'find ourselves' spiritually by following our interests and expressing our individuality as fully as we can.

Not that there's anything wrong with doing what we love and being successful at it, or being known for what we do. The problem arises when we believe that the fulfillment of the material self we're projecting equates to spiritual awakening. Improving the self and finding the Self is not the same thing, and while the first could possibly lead to the second, it's far more likely to lead us away from the Self.

When Jesus said we must know ourselves, he was talking about the true Self. How do we come to know and understand something that we've been completely unaware of? We can begin taking a closer look at how the self hides the Self. The self is known through perception, the Self through vision. Perception looks out at the world, vision looks within. Since birth we've taken the reality of this world for granted since we had no reason to think otherwise. We've never doubted that the tree in our front yard, on even the yard itself, were there even when we weren't looking at them. But quantum physics tells us our world is constructed of interconnected energy patterns, not separate forms.

When consciousness is directed at energy patterns, they're picked up by the senses and then filtered through the brain and the emotions. It's actually impossible to touch, hear, smell, taste or see anything; the sensations we believe we're experiencing have always had their origin in the brain. But the brain and emotions filter out a large percentage of what we're exposed to. After that, the brain goes through a selective process of editing and modifying that input. Generally it keeps what fits with the data it's already compiled, and discards new ideas that challenge the status quo. For these reasons, science is now realizing it's impossible for truth or objective reality to exist in our world.

When we say everything in the material world exists as an interference pattern until consciousness is directed at it, this includes your body. Even the personality amounts to little more than a construct made up of a combination of what others tell us and the stories we tell ourselves. That means the material 'you' doesn't actually exist. Who are you? The observer that projects the image; the pure, non-local consciousness that permeates the quantum field.

Vision vs. Perception

When Jesus told his followers to "fast from the world," he was encouraging them to starve out perception. This includes letting go of the belief that anything in this world is real. In one of Jesus' more cryptic sayings in the Greek version of *Thomas,* his disciples asked him, "When will you be revealed to us and when shall we see you?" Evidently they recognized there was much more to Jesus than met the eye and they wanted him to divulge what made him seem so different. Jesus told them his identity would be revealed, "When you strip off your clothing and are not ashamed." Jesus was not asking his followers to literally strip. Instead, he was using clothing as a symbol for the body. And even though he was asking them to take off the body, this didn't mean that it would take their death for them to understand him.

Jesus was asking his followers to figure out who they were without the body or personality. When they could strip away everything external to the true Self, they would finally understand who Jesus was and who they were. Jesus knew that at that point they would know there was no difference between them, but until that happened he would *appear* to be very different.

Why? Buddha had the same experience as Jesus, and the seeming difference was explained this way, "When people asked the Buddha if he was a god or an angel, he smiled and said, 'I am awake.'"

The only difference between a Jesus or a Buddha and the rest of humanity is that Jesus and Buddha have already stripped away the false self and woke up from the dream of separation. They appear to be god-like, but in truth, we are all God. This is why Jesus said, "Know what is before your face and what is hidden from you will be disclosed to you. For there is nothing hidden that will not become apparent." Jesus was standing before them, stripped of all but Self. If they understood what was right before them, nothing would be hidden. The Self knows everything we need to know. When we trade the self for the Self, perception for vision, we 'know,' which eliminates any need for beliefs. And when we know, we no longer fit into the false mind's image of humanity. Since the false mind can't cope with this, it engineers a story to explain the difference. This story turns a human spiritual master into a god or savior and creates an unbreachable chasm between us.

Jesus identified this difference when he said, "I am the one who comes from what is whole...For this reason I say, if one is whole, one will be filled with light, but if one is divided, one will be filled with darkness." To really understand our innate oneness, we must fast from the world's insistence that we are separate and strip off our attachment to the illusionary bodies and personalities the false self has constructed in its pursuit of specialness. We continue to use the body and personality to navigate our way through the material world, but we do so as an observer, or as Jesus said, "be passersby."

Liberation

Chapter Six

What Is the Kingdom?

When we see Jesus as human, we understand that he was not speaking to his followers from a lofty position. He had gone through the same transition from false self to true Self that he was encouraging them to undertake. From experience, he realized it's challenging for anyone to give up their attachment to the false self and the world it projects until they begin to get a glimpse of who and what they actually are. Here is the surprising information he shared:

> *If your leaders say to you, "Look, the kingdom is in heaven," then the birds of heaven will precede you. If they say to you "It is in the sea," then the fish will precede you. Rather, God's kingdom is inside you and outside you. Whoever knows oneself will find this. And when you know yourselves, you will understand that you are children of the living Father. But if you do not know yourselves, you are in poverty, and you are poverty.*

Jesus' followers must have felt extremely confused when he said the kingdom is inside and outside each of us. The Jewish people felt sure God's kingdom was a heavenly government that existed outside the material universe. They expected that any kingdom God would establish on earth would be an extension of that heavenly government, a literal political entity, a theocracy ruled by someone God had chosen. Of course many Jews were fervently expecting God to appoint a warrior king to deliver them from the Romans, but some Jews expected a cosmic warrior who would restore the equilibrium between good and evil earth wide. Regardless, the Jews thought of God's kingdom as a literal government. As long as they continued to think a kingdom and a government had to be synonymous, they would misunderstand what Jesus was telling them.

Understanding the 'Quantum' Kingdom

Jesus' direct experience of the Divine taught him that God's kingdom is not a political structure. But a kingdom can also be defined as "An area or sphere where one holds a preeminent position." Jesus understood the oneness of All That Is; he knew that there was no place in the universe where the Divine was not, and that certainly qualifies as a preeminent position. The universe operates within certain parameters, but these 'laws' have no resemblance to the legal system of a government. The Divine operates from love and has no need or desire to control, limit or enforce the religious or moral codes many take so seriously. Most religions paint a picture of God as a ruler demanding obedience, but that concept is an insult to Source. When you *are* everything, what would you rule over and how would you govern yourself?

The quantum model of the indivisible oneness of the universe agrees with Jesus' summary, "God's kingdom is inside you and outside you." We are always within the kingdom, and the kingdom is always within us. As Buckminster Fuller noted, "You cannot got out of the universe. The universe is not a system. The universe is not a shape. The universe is a scenario. You are always in universe. You can only get out of systems." Quantum physics has shown us that everything in existence is an indivisible, interconnected part of the whole, so the bodies we project are certainly part of God's kingdom. But when Jesus told his followers the kingdom was inside and outside them, he was thinking on a far grander scale.

The creation story in Genesis says that Adam and Eve were made in the image of God. This is confusing since Adam was made of dust, was mortal and quickly proved his imperfection by disobeying his creator. Regardless, the genealogy found in the New Testament gospel of Luke traces Jesus' ancestry back to Adam. Logic would say that this chain of events made Adam the direct creation of God and Jesus a human. The institutionalized Christian church later decided only Jesus' body had descended from Adam but he was actually a spirit creature, the only 'son' directly begotten by God. Due to this special relationship, God stopped creating and all other creations came through Jesus. This turns the tables and makes Jesus the father of Adam and all his descendants. But the Jesus depicted in *Thomas* disagreed with all these ideas and indicated that something even greater was meant by the Genesis statement claiming we were made in God's image.

In God's Image

Since it's impossible for a mortal, material body to be in God's immortal, nonmaterial image, many have concluded that this means there is another part of us that resembles God, something we call the soul. But you'll see as we go further into the chapter that Jesus had something even more literal in mind. He told his followers they were not mere material or spiritual images of God, but direct creations made from the stuff of God, the "children of the living Father." To understand this, we'll need to look further into the methods Jesus suggested his followers use to discover their true identity. Again, discovering the meaning of Jesus' saying is necessary, but the brain's logic is not the key to understanding Jesus' symbolic language. Instead, we must be willing to quiet the false mind's chatter so that we can be instructed by the One Mind. Jesus said:

Have you discovered the beginning, then, so that you are seeking the end? For where the beginning is the end will be. Blessed is one who stands at the beginning: that one will know the end and will not taste death.

This statement would be impossible to understand if we insist on thinking of the birth of the body as our beginning. Although many Christians believe that humans were angels in heaven before being born on earth, the Bible itself doesn't support that view. However, Jesus was inferring that we had a far more interesting beginning than human birth. To discern what Jesus' meant we'll look at several more verses found in the Greek and Coptic versions of *Thomas*:

> *Jesus said, "When you strip without being ashamed and you take your clothes and put them under your feet like little children and trample them, then you will see the child of the living one and you will not be afraid.*
>
> *Jesus says, "Where there are three, they are without God and where there is only one, I say I am with that one. (Greek)*
>
> *On the day when you were one, you became two. But when you become two, what will you do?*
>
> *Jesus said to them, "When you make the two into one and when you make the inner*

> *like the outer and outer like the inner. . . then you will enter the kingdom.*
>
> *Jesus said, "If you bring forth what is within you, what you have will save you."*

At first these verses sound quite odd and appear to have no relationship, but there is a significant connection:

> *Jesus said, "When you strip without being ashamed and you take your clothes and put them under your feet like little children and trample them, then you will see the child of the living one and you will not be afraid.*

In this first verse, Jesus again used the symbol of clothing to stand for the body. Young children have not yet been conditioned to the social constraints that cause us to feel shame over nakedness. They also have great disdain for anything that restrains or constricts them, so it's common to see them pulling off their shoes or clothes. Jesus used this word picture because he wanted his followers to make the connection that the body is actually a constraint that keeps us from recognizing our true identity.

We can take this verse in two ways. Ultimately it refers to escaping the cycle of birth and death that keeps us tied to virtual reality. When we're ready to stop projecting the drama we call life, we're free to wake once more in oneness. At that point, there will be no doubt that each of us is "the child of the living one." But even before we're ready for that ultimate awakening, we can begin letting go of our attachment to the body and personality.

As we let go of perception, our vision improves and we see ourselves and the universe in an entirely different way. As we understand just how meaningless the body and personality are in relation to reality, we'll happily begin stripping off our attachment to our false identity and trample it beneath our feet. This doesn't mean that we need to disdain, harm or deprive the body; after all, it's still part of Divine existence. The body itself is not the issue; it's only our belief that we *are* the body and our attachment to it that causes us to miss the oneness of all things.

Oneness

Jesus says, "Where there are three, they are without God and where there is only one, I say I am with that one. (Greek)

In the second verse, Jesus alludes to oneness as our original state, but makes the point that something disturbed that oneness and needs to be corrected. When Jesus said, "Where there are three, they are without God" he uses 'three' to signify duality. In duality there must be a 'you' to be a 'me,' but he adds the third to symbolize a god that is separate. Then he adds that Source does not participate in our dualistic dream of separation and specialness. Most of Jesus' followers were either unable or unwilling to accept this, and it still sounds shocking to many invested in institutionalized Christianity. But the Divine cannot exist in conflict, and quantum discoveries tell us only oneness exists. Any Gods that are based on duality are an invention of the false mind. On the other hand, "where there is only one, I say I am with that one." When Jesus stopped thinking in dualistic terms and embraced oneness, the Divine became accessible to him once again, and the same is true for us.

> *On the day when you were one, you became two. But when you become two, what will you do?*

In the third verse, Jesus poses a question everyone will eventually have to answer, "On the day when you were one, you became two. But when you become two, what will you do?" A quick look at the world tells us separation has taken us to the brink of world disaster. We continue to hear scientists, politicians, economists, ecologists, educators and religious leaders all telling us that we won't be able to find a solution to world problems until we're willing to work together. Unfortunately, they don't understand that duality prevents that from happening. The flawed foundation of the false mind's thought system can only be jettisoned, not repaired. That's why Jesus was moved to say, "I found them all drunk, and I did not find any of them thirsty. My soul ached for the children of humanity, because they are blind in their hearts and do not see, for they came into the world empty, and they also seek to depart from the world empty."

> *Jesus said to them, "When you make the two into one and when you make the inner*

> *like the outer and outer like the inner. . .
> then you will enter the kingdom.*

In the fourth verse, Jesus explains the solution to the problem when he encourages his followers to" make the two into one" once more. In other words, stop thinking in dualistic terms and embrace the oneness of all things. This goes much farther than just repeating the idea, it means living it in every way we can. We can think of making the inner like the outer in two ways. On one hand, we can be consistent, having no conflict between our thoughts and actions. Or, we can think of it as bringing the personality in line with the true Self. Of course the kingdom is outside and inside us whether we are aware of it or not, but we haven't really 'entered' it until we're awake enough to see it, or as Jesus put it, we "shake off [the] wine." But this means returning to our original state by letting go of the false mind's dualistic thought system and "Make the two into one…the inner like the outer."

From self to Self

> *Jesus said, "If you bring forth what is within you, what you have will save you."*

In the fifth verse, Jesus makes it clear that we're saved not by worship, works, sacrifice or obedience. Instead, "If you bring forth what is within you, what you have will save you." This saying comes from one who looked inside and discovered we all have within us everything we need to return to oneness. Instead of putting our faith in someone outside us and making them our savior, we all have the responsibility of saving ourselves. When the body is asleep someone else may try to wake us up, but it is always the body itself that must do the waking. We chose to project the dream of separation, and we're the only ones who can choose when we've had enough of dreams and are ready to wake up.

In the gnostic *Dialogue of the Savior*, Jesus' followers asked him to reveal the source of his teaching. Knowing he differed from them only in the level of their understanding, he answered, "Light the lamp within you...Knock on yourself as upon a door and walk upon yourself as on a straight road." If they would do this, they would discover that they were God's kingdom, just as we are. Jesus was a person of his times, and he used the term 'kingdom' because it was something his followers were focused on. But

Jesus used the term to steer his followers far away from the concept of a literal government that would rule and protect them. Instead, he wanted them to understand that God's kingdom is a state of being that encompasses All That Is. The kingdom is everywhere because the Divine is everywhere, and in a very real sense, you and not just an image of the Divine, *you are the Divine*. In the next two chapters, we'll look at our quantum universe to discover exactly what that means.

Chapter Seven

Here, There, Everywhere

Quantum physicists are just beginning to fully appreciate what Jesus meant when he said, "Lift up the stone, and you will find me there. Split the piece of wood, and I am there." This verse refers to something physicists describe as the 'non-local' nature of the universe. What is meant by non-local?

Non-local Reality

In the visible world we expect to find things in specific locations. Even if a car is speeding down the road, each second it travels it's in another specific location. We use maps, directions and addresses to describe these specific locations, but physicists found that it was impossible to map specific locations for subatomic packets of energy called photons. Why? Photons have the qualities of both a particle and a wave, and are constantly in motion. Physicists were shocked to realize that unlike material objects, a photon's location and velocity could not both be known at the same time. If the location was pinpointed, the velocity became uncertain. If the velocity was known, the location became uncertain. At the quantum level, energy has only a potential to be somewhere, making it impossible to say exactly where anything is.

When physicists create abstract mathematical formulas to describe the possible location of a photon, they call it a "probability wave" since the location is only probable, not factual. We can visualize this phenomenon by imagining being in a completely dark cave where no light can enter. Now think of someone walking around in the cave, turning a flashlight on and off intermittently. When the light flashes, it's like the photon in particle form. When the light is off, it resembles the photon in wave form. Since you can't see the person, you have no way of predicting where the flash will appear next. Like the physicist, you can only make an estimate of a probable next location. Since no specific address or locality can be assigned to subatomic particles, and since they could be anywhere, we must think of them as 'non-local.'

Holographic film demonstrates this same non-local quality. Before the days of digital cameras film was sent to a processor who returned your pictures along with a 'negative' image of each photo. If you wanted to make duplicates of a picture of a sailboat you had taken, they could be reproduced from the negative. You could cut the negative in half and still have pictures printed, but each half would only produce a picture of the part of the boat that appeared on that piece of the negative.

We learned earlier that holographic film is very different from photographic film. Instead of displaying the image that's projected from it, the image is spread over the surface of the film in an interference pattern that looks like ripples that spread out and intersect when raindrops hit a pond. That means that the information needed to project a 3D holographic image is spread throughout the film. You could cut the film in several pieces and still project the entire image from each piece. The information spread throughout the film is 'non-local' because it's impossible to locate any of it on the film. We could say that it's nowhere and everywhere at the same time. When we say the quantum universe is interconnected, it's a serious understatement because, like the holographic film, everything *is* everywhere. Jesus was speaking quite literally when he said, "Lift up the stone, and you will find me there. Split the piece of wood, and I am there."

In an earlier chapter we quoted a verse from the ancient *Brihadaranyaka Upanishad* that also points to the non-local quality of the universe. As we look at it again, ask yourself where you would locate the lump of salt once it's been dissolved in water:

> *As a lump of salt thrown in water dissolves and cannot be taken out again . . . the separate self dissolves in the sea of pure consciousness, infinite and immortal. Separateness arises from identifying the Self with the body, which is made up of the elements; when this physical identification dissolves, there can be no more separate self.*

Before the salt goes into the water, we can see it and name its location. Once the salt has dissolved into the water, it's impossible to locate. But that doesn't mean it no longer exists or is no longer salt; it's still salt, but it has become non-local. Like salt in water, everything in quantum oneness is here, there and everywhere at once.

What Is 'the Void?'

Since we're used to separate forms and the parameters that govern our 'local' world, our true existence in non-local oneness may sound quite frightening. That may especially be true if we imagine it to mean the loss of self-identity or entering a 'void' of non-existence. In this book, we've spoken many times of letting go of our attachment to the body and personality, but when we do that, we don't fade into nothingness, we wake up to our true Self. We're letting go of something that's valueless in exchange for something that's beyond value. This exchange has often been misunderstood, and fearful, because Eastern philosophies often speak of the Divine as a 'void.'

In the West we do think of a void as 'nothingness,' but that would be an incorrect interpretation of the Eastern meaning. Instead, void would more correctly be understood as space. We could think of All That Is as 'void' of duality since it contains only the Divine. But in the Eastern sense, space symbolizes something that's void of objects but filled with energy that has the potential of becoming anything consciousness can imagine. Instead of thinking of it as an empty bowl, you could imagine it as a bowl filled with all the ingredients you would need to make a cake. The ingredients haven't been stirred, poured into a pan or baked yet, so they exist as 'potential.' The ingredients aren't cake yet, but that doesn't make the bowl empty. Potential is everything and nothing all at the same time.

The fact that consciousness, life and energy form the foundation of the universe demonstrates that we need never fear that oneness is a void of emptiness. Instead, The Divine not only contains everything in existence, but the potential for everything that could ever exist. Alan Watts observed, "It is the great and imaginary terror of Western man that nothingness will be the permanent end of the universe. We do not easily grasp the point that the void is creative, and that being comes from non-being as sound from silence and light from space." This is beautifully illustrated by that ancient Taoist sage, Lao Tzu:

Thirty spokes unite at the wheel's hub;

It is the center hole that makes it useful.

Shape clay into a vessel,

It is the space within that makes it useful.

Cut out doors and windows for a room;

It is the holes which make it useful.

Therefore profit comes from what is there;

Usefulness from what is not there.

Your Creative Reality

When we understand that the universe holds the tools of consciousness and energy potential, we realize that it is the foundation of all creativity. We also realize these tools make this a universe of free will, choice and imagination. Most religions assume that these qualities should be hoarded by the Divine. The Bible story of Adam and Eve recorded in Genesis and the story told in the book of Job about Satan's rebellion, highlight the idea that free will in the hands of anyone but God is a very dangerous tool. But quantum research has a very different story to tell. As we learned earlier, even the tiniest photon can consciously interact with researchers to provide the result they expect. Clearly, we all have the gift of free will and choice or we wouldn't have the opportunity to experiment with separation and specialness. Although the Bible claims that we're paying a terrible price for the misuse of free will, it's impossible to imagine that the Divine would give us a gift that would be so powerful we could rip the oneness of All That Is into pieces. Such a 'gift' would allow us to destroy the universe, and in turn, destroy the Divine. This hasn't happened, and never will. When we wake up, we'll see that we've tried something that doesn't work, but there's no punishment involved for having tried it.

Instead of losing ourselves in oneness, we'll discover who we actually are and have the opportunity to reach our *full* creative potential. Even in our virtual reality we still possess creativity, but it cannot begin to compare with the level of creativity possible to our true Self. The things we've made in this world can leave us in awe, but they pale in comparison to what can be created with consciousness and energy. And as non-local beings, we'll have the unique opportunity to experience through whatever we create. Instead of sitting outside our creations, we will continue to be one with them just as the Divine permeates everything in existence.

Unique Within Equality

There is no need to equate oneness with sameness, just as there would be no point in having several children if you thought they would all be exactly alike. If we fearfully equate oneness with the loss of personal identity, it helps to remember that Jesus told his followers when they 'woke up,' they would realize they were "children of the living Father." Each facet of a diamond is different from the others around it; still, they are all one when we look at the diamond as a whole.

It would be impossible for us to have a relationship with the Divine if either we, or the Divine, had no individuality or personality. And as we discussed earlier, the Divine created us so that we could enjoy a loving relationship, not dissolve into nothingness. We've learned that the Divine cannot exist divided, and so oneness remains even though we dream and project our experiment in separation and specialness. But we can't expect to have a fulfilling relationship with the Divine while we're asleep any more than we can enjoy our friends and family while we're taking a nap.

Those who have experienced the Divine directly have always reported that the defining characteristic of Source is love. The gnostic writer Valentinus tells us the Divine "was all love and love is not love if there is nothing to be loved." Rumi calls us "the beloved of the Beloved" and says, "Listen, and your whole life will become a conversation in thought and act between you and Him, directly, wordlessly, now and always. It was to enjoy this conversation that you and I were created."

Since the brain and the senses can't comprehend existing in non-local oneness, it's understandable that the concept is frightening. As a defense, the brain concocts stories about heavens and hells that are filled with separate forms and the same old concepts of separation and specialness that serve as the foundation for this world. When we experience the Divine directly, we understand non-local oneness as our natural state.

Here, There, Everywhere

Chapter Eight

Beings of Light

As Jesus opened the minds of his followers to their true identity, he mentioned another truth that science is beginning to figure out. Jesus had just told a woman named Salome, "I am the one who comes from what is whole," but then added, "For this reason I say, 'If one is whole, one will be filled with light. But if one is divided, one will be filled with darkness.'" Few things are mentioned in connection with the Divine as often as love and light. Since we can express love, we appreciate it more readily. But light can tell us a great deal about the Divine, the universe and our own nature. Light has several meanings in spiritual teachings, but science has recently contributed information that can take our understanding of Divine light to a new level.

In the Bible, the contrast between light and darkness is often used to symbolize the duality of good and evil. John 3:20, 21 reads in part, "For everyone who does evil hates the light...But he who does what is true comes to the light."

Light is also used as a metaphor for God's word as Psalm 119:105 makes clear, "Your word is a lamp to my feet and a light to my path." And Jesus' famous Sermon on the Mount likens light to good works that reflect God's love, "You are the light of the world...Let your light so shine before men, that they may see your good works and give glory to your Father in heaven." (Matthew 5: 14-16)

Divine Light

In gnostic writings, the Divine is often described as a 'life-giving, perfect light.' *The Secret Book of John* explains, "The One is the immeasurable light. . .Not that the One possesses this. Rather, the One gives immeasurable and incomprehensible light." The gnostic view that light and life are synonymous is also reflected in the Katha Upanishad, "There shines not the sun, neither moon nor star, nor flash of lightning, nor fire lit on earth. The Self is the light reflected by all. [Source] is shining, everything shines after him." Science is now recognizing that these sayings are far more than platitudes, in fact, light and life are inseparable.

We usually think about light in terms of the energy that's released from stars and illuminates the universe. The creation story in Genesis tells us God said, "Let there be light" and thereafter, light separated the day from the night. But the light spiritual masters spoke of was something completely different. It's becoming more and more evident to scientists that quantum light serves as the foundation or matrix for the material portion of the universe.

In the previous chapter we made a comment about the 'fullness' of the so-called empty space that appears to take up 2/3 of the universe. Scientists once believed this space was filled with something they called 'ether,' then they thought it might be a vacuum. But now research has demonstrated it's a quantum light field they call the 'zero-point field.' This field is so potent; the energy contained in a single cubic meter has the potential to boil all the water in the oceans of the world.

The zero-point field appears to be much more than a place for the warehousing of quantum energy. Classical physics assumed that all matter had mass. Mass can be thought of as the amount of resistance an object has to acceleration. The more mass, the less acceleration and vice versa. This appears to be correct because the force needed to throw a bowling ball far exceeds the force needed to throw a ping pong ball. But as we've learned, the seemingly solid, stable world of matter is really an energy field that doesn't innately possess mass. New quantum theories propose that mass is an illusion created by the light energy of the zero-point field as it opposes acceleration. Simply put, the universe is built on a foundation of life-giving quantum light that has all the properties needed to create and sustain the illusion of our virtual reality.

A Very Different Light

This theory finds surprising support in an ancient Jewish manuscript called the *Haggadah*, which reads, "The light created at the very beginning is not the same light emitted by the sun, the moon and the stars, which appeared on the fourth day." The early gnostic writing, *Creation of the World and the Alien Man* agrees, saying, "There is no boundary for the light and it was not known when it came into being. Nothing was when light was not, nothing was when radiance was not. Nothing was when the Mighty Life was not, there never was a boundary for the light."

Scientists have also discovered that tiny particles of light, called biophotons, are emitted by all living things. In the *Gospel of Thomas*, Jesus took this description a step further when he recognized the Divine quality of light, and told his followers they were part of that Divine light. He said, "If they say to you, 'Where have you come from?' Say to them, 'We have come from the light, from the place where the light came into being by itself, established itself, and became manifest through their image.' If they say to you, 'Is it you?' say, 'We are its children, and we are the chosen of the living Father.'" Now we see that the universe permeated with consciousness, energy and light is synonymous with the Divine, and we are one with the Divine. Instead of being the material image of a creator God that's separate from us, we are the very *being* of our Source.

Unfortunately, we rarely recognize this Divine light in ourselves or others. When Jesus said, "For this reason I say, if one is whole, one will be filled with light, but if one is divided, one will be filled with darkness," he wasn't using darkness as a symbol of evil. Instead he meant that our desire for separation had blinded us to oneness and left us in spiritual darkness.

The gnostic *Dialogue of the Savior* agreed saying, "As long as your hearts are dark, your light...is far from you." That's why Jesus told his followers, "No one lights a lamp and puts it under a basket, nor does one put it in a hidden place. Rather, one puts it on a stand so that all who come and go will see its light." Many interpret Jesus words as an admonition to use your talents for good, but when we realize that we are actually *beings* of light, we understand that he wanted us to recognize and reveal our true identity. No matter what we achieve as the self, it pales in comparison to this realization.

Even so, the Divine light we radiate in this world is a reflection, not the light itself. Our inability to see ourselves as we actually are has not dimmed our light. We remain as we always have been: beings of Divine light. Now that light is a reflection only because physical eyes are unable to see it. Regardless, we can still radiate and reflect the light of Divine love. As Rumi pointed out, "You think you are earthly beings, but you have been kneaded from the Light of Certainty. You are the guardians of God's Light, so come, return to the root of the root of your own Self."

Know *Your* Light

Jesus recognized the futile cycle we create when we give away our power and believe in our own emptiness. His longing to help 'wake up' everyone he spoke to is evident in his words, "My soul ached for the children of humanity, because they are blind in their hearts and do not see, for they came into the world empty, and they also seek to depart from the world empty." Jesus saved himself by looking within and discovering that he was not the body or personality society had created for him. As he began to understand his true identity, he willingly strengthened his connection with the One Mind we share with All That Is. He saw the universe in a very different way and began to live a new life.

Jesus' light shone very brightly. Many were drawn to him, and he could have accomplished a great deal on the earth, but he understood the futility of trying to build on a flawed foundation. Instead, when circumstances brought him to suffering he used the opportunity to show in an undeniable manner that suffering and death are an illusion. As the writer of *Thomas* pointed out, the words he recorded are the sayings of the "living Jesus."

The words are still meant to be interactive. They can still serve as a jumping off point for your own inner exploration. The living Jesus is still available to meet you in oneness.

It would be impossible for our experiment with separation and specialness to cause a rift between us and our Source since oneness can't be divided in reality. We were given free will and a safe way to use it. There is no punishment involved in this experiment. As the gnostic writer of the *Gospel of Philip* explained, "When the pearl is cast down into the mud, it does not become greatly despised...but it always has value in the eyes of its owner. Compare the sons of God, wherever they may be. They still have value in the eyes of their Father." No matter how long we linger in our illusion, Rumi assures us, "There is a rope of light between your heart and Source that nothing can weaken or break, and it is always in His hands."

Beings of Light

Chapter Nine

Two Masters

The New Testament gospels include two sayings that point out the difficulty of living in conflict. Most of us are familiar with Matthew 6:24, "No one can serve two masters; for either he will hate the one and love the other, or he will be devoted to the one and despise the other. You cannot serve God and riches." Luke 16:10-13 is far more detailed. It reads, "He who is faithful in a very little is faithful also in much; and he who is dishonest in a very little is dishonest also in much. If then you have not been faithful in the unrighteous riches, who will entrust to you the true riches? And if you have not been faithful in that which is another's who will give you that which is your own? No servant can serve two masters; for either he will hate the one and love the other, or he will be devoted to the one and despise the other. You cannot serve God and riches."

Although the writer of Luke equates the conflict between two masters with faithlessness, both Matthew and Luke are focused on the conflict between God and money. We could easily imagine money as a symbol for the secular world in general, but several other verses demonstrate that money was used literally rather than symbolically. 1Timothy 3: 2, 3 reads, "Now a bishop must be above reproach...no drunkard, not violent but gentle, not quarrelsome, and no lover of money." Hebrews 13:5 recommends, "Keep your life free from love of money, and be content with what you have." 1Timothy 6:10 goes even further and says, "For the love of money is the root of all evils; it is through this craving that some have wandered away from the faith and pierced their hearts with many pangs."

In Matthew 19: 16-23 a story is told about a young man who approached Jesus and asked what he must do to have eternal life. After the young man claimed that he was already following all the commandments of Moses, Jesus told him to sell his belongings, give the proceeds to the poor and join him. This grieved the young man because he was wealthy. After he left, Jesus told his followers, "Truly I say to you, it will be hard for a rich man to enter the kingdom of heaven. Again, I tell you, it is easier for a camel to go through the eye of a needle than for a rich man to enter the kingdom of God."

Of course the absurd picture of a camel trying to get through the eye of a literal needle pops into our mind, and we instantly come to the conclusion that wealth absolutely precludes any chance of awakening spiritually. But the 'Needle's Eye' may have been the name of a small gate within a much larger city gate. For a caravan of traders that wanted to enter the city after dark when the larger gates had been closed, this posed a problem. The camel's burdens would have to be unloaded on one side of the gate and reloaded after they had moved through the gate. But the real difficulty was that the camel would have to kneel to get through, something that a camel would not be inclined to do. It would no doubt be assumed by Jesus' listeners that it was a very greedy trader who would be so eager for business they would drive their camels late into the night and not want to wait until the larger gates opened in the morning to begin trading. If we think of a literal camel and needle, the rich man would have no chance. If the 'needle's eye' was a smaller gate, it would be difficult, but certainly far from impossible. Regardless, these verses have caused many Christians to live extremely austere lives, mistakenly thinking a life of deprivation would win God's favor. This happened because the sayings were transformed into rules.

Making Rules

When "No one can serve two masters" is connected to "You can't serve God and riches" we're confronted with an either/or situation: serve God or serve money. This connection transformed a wisdom saying into a rule about money Christians believed they must obey. Then, instead of using the wisdom sayings for inner contemplation, readers became fixated on the rule and how it should govern the actions of the body. Instead of examining their own inner motivation, they became concerned over the outward appearance of their relationship with money. Rules become a slippery slope that blinds us to inner motivation.

The rules and regulations Jesus is said to have handed out in the New Testament are completely incompatible with a saying we considered earlier in *Thomas*. As you'll remember, when Jesus' disciples asked him for instructions concerning fasting, praying and charitable giving, Jesus replied, "Do not lie and do not do what you hate." Of course this advice directed them to look into their own heart to discern their motivations but said nothing about the body's actions. This concept is reinforced in the gnostic *Gospel of Mary* where Jesus warned his followers, "do not lay down any rule…nor promulgate law like the lawgiver or else you might be dominated by it." Most Christians have been taught to associate 'sin' with breaking rules and moral codes, but when Peter asked Jesus in the *Gospel of Mary*, "What is the sin of the world?" Jesus replied, "There is no such thing as a sin" and explained, "This is why you get sick and die; because you love what deceives you."

What Is Your Heart's Desire?

From a quantum standpoint, money is no more than a thought. Like everything else that we project in our dualistic virtual reality, money is just one more thing that we can use to support our belief in separation and specialness if that is our choice. In and of itself, it's impossible for money to be good or bad, or even the love of money to be either right or wrong. However, there is no denying the truth of Jesus' words at Matthew 6: 21, "For where you treasure is, there will your heart be also." Jesus wasn't saying we couldn't have things. Rather, *it is far more important how we feel about those things.*

Jesus illustrated this point by saying, "The father's kingdom is like a merchant who had a supply of merchandise and then found a pearl. That merchant was prudent; he sold the merchandise and bought the single pearl for himself. So also with you, see His treasure that is unfailing, that is enduring, where no moth comes to devour and no worm destroys." When the merchant became aware of the pearl, everything else he owned lost its luster. Now the only thing in his heart became the pearl. Like the merchant, when we experience the Divine, the things we have in this world lose their value. We can continue to have and enjoy them, but we no longer put value on them. Wherever our thoughts are, our heart follows. This is beautifully expressed in the *Birhadaranyaka Upanishad*:

You are what your deep, driving desire is.

As you desire is, so is your will.

As your will is, so is your deed.

As your deed is, so is your destiny.

No matter what the actions of the body appear to be, they are following the deep desires of the heart. Neurosceintists have discovered the heart has its own intelligence that rivals the brain. Scientists have understood for some time that the brain sends signals to all parts of the body, but they're just beginning to understand that the heart also sends signals to the brain. The discovery they found most surprising was that the heart is selective and doesn't automatically obey the brain's commands. But when the heart sends a message to the brain, the brain obeys and the body follows. When we let go of the false self, our thinking is transferred from the brain and false mind to the One Mind we share with Source. Since the One Mind and the heart have the same desires, we are then in harmony.

We once overheard a conversation between a woman who regularly served meals at a homeless shelter and a friend. She was telling the friend how much she detested the homeless and hated every moment she was at the shelter. When the friend suggested she stop going, she explained that the shelter was the favorite charity of the president of the company where she worked. She was volunteering there because she was determined to become a major player at the company and knew her work at the shelter would impress her boss. Clearly the woman was driven by her desire, and no matter how many times she went through the action of being of service to others, her heart was closed to anything outside that focus. For her, the pearl was professional and financial success.

Free Will

We could easily judge this woman and decide she was heartless, but then we would be forgetting that we were all given free will by Source *plus* the opportunity to express it any way we wish within virtual reality. It's true that everything we think and do will take us either farther into separation or closer to oneness, but none of our choices are condemned. At times, taking an experience as far as we can in what appears to others to be a very negative direction, may end up teaching us more about the emptiness of our illusion than trying to live a balanced or a more positive life. The Divine is fully aware of this and allows us to follow our heart where ever it may take us. Our 'pearl' can be anything we choose, valuable or valueless. These thoughts may be very difficult to accept by many who see God and Jesus as law givers and enforcers. The gnostic gospels ask us to look at Jesus and Source in a completely different way.

Ultimate Reality created parameters that govern the operation of the universe and guarantee the survival of All That Is. These parameters are what we might think of as the 'Laws of Nature' since they govern the operation of the universe. As we've learned, the 'laws' that govern the visible portion of the universe are very different from those that govern the invisible, quantum portion. This makes sense because a 'law' like gravity is essential for us, but useless and unnecessary in non-local oneness. Although scientists are a long way from discovering or understanding these laws, it's obvious they work for the good of everything in existence. However, it's important to understand that these parameters have no connection with the laws, rules or moral codes that are meant to regulate human behavior in virtual reality. Although humans regularly claim that God has dictated the religious rules and moral codes that humans must follow, our free will would be invalidated if that were the case. (Not to mention the fact that there is very little agreement on what those 'rules' or 'laws' actually are.)

No matter what we do, it would be impossible for us to overstep the parameters set by Source. We are a thought in the Mind of God, and as such, we do not have the power or ability to do anything that would cause real harm. But within the parameters set by Source, we have the free will to make choices even when they are not in our best interest. If that was not the case, we wouldn't be able to project separation, specialness and the misery that is innate to that thought system.

Free will also means that the Divine does not interfere in our dream unless we wake up to the Self and live from a place of oneness with Source. At that point we cannot label it interference since we've invited the Divine into our heart. The rules and laws of this world are the concepts and projections of the false mind. As such, they serve the purpose of protecting and enforcing the thought system of the false mind. Although every religion claims that their 'holy' books were inspired by God and their religious rules and moral codes are God's will, they are actually the product of the false mind. Some books that are now considered 'holy' or inspired are based on the teachings of a spiritual master like Jesus who did experience the Divine directly. But it's important to remember that the person who wrote down the information likely did not. It's inevitable that they interpreted what they saw and heard through their own thought system. Some of what they have written may be accurate; other things may be colored by their preconceived notions, attachments and aversions.

If the writer also experienced the Divine directly, their words will carry more of the correct meaning the master was trying to convey, but either way, there are no 'holy books' dictated by God. Even if the spiritual master wrote down the words themselves, they are still telling their personal experience of the Divine, not giving out Divine mandates. This is not to say that we can't benefit from reading these works, just that we need to keep in mind how they came into being. This information may be upsetting, but it's also liberating. Instead of trying to live up to a document that may make little sense in our day, it frees us to find out for ourselves what the Divine wants to tell us personally. It also explains why there are so many 'holy books' and religions that differ so widely and contradict one another. This is also why the gnostic gospels sound so very different than the New Testament gospels.

As we wake up to our true identity, we become the love, joy and peace that the Divine is, and live from that place. At that point, no rules are necessary. We may speak of 'the law of love,' but this is a way of life directed by a love that contains no rules. As Thomas Aquinas said, "Love, and do what you will." This is possible because when we're in harmony with Divine love, we can do no harm. Our actions may look strange or rebellious to those who live according to man-made rules, but they are perfectly understandable from the perspective of love and oneness.

The 'Two Masters' in *Thomas*

As you'll see, there is no mention of riches when Jesus tells the parable of two masters in *Thomas*, but there is additional information that gives a very different perspective:

> *Jesus said, "A person cannot mount two horses or bend two bows. And a servant cannot serve two masters, or that servant will honor the one and offend the other. No person drinks aged wine and*

immediately desires to drink new wine. New wine is not poured into aged wineskins, or they might break, and aged wine is not poured into a new wineskin, or it might spoil. An old patch is not sewn onto a new garment, for there would be a tear."

The additional sayings about wine, wineskins and garments are also recorded in the New Testament at Matthew 9:16, 17 but they are not associated with the saying about two masters recorded at Matthew 6:24. Instead, they are associated with a question that was asked by some of the disciples of John the Baptizer in verse 14, "Then the disciples of John came to him, saying, 'Why do we and the Pharisees fast, but your disciples do not fast?'" In verses 16 and 17, Jesus answers, "And no one puts a piece of unshrunk cloth on an old garment, for the patch tears away from the garment, and a worse tear is made. Neither is new wine put into old wineskins; if it is, the skins burst, and the wine is spilled, and the skins are destroyed; but new wine is put into fresh wineskins, and so both are preserved."

In *Thomas*, Jesus' words are not preceded by a question from John's disciples, but that question can help us with the words in *Thomas*. John's disciples were still following the Jewish laws, which included fasting. They had not made any real changes in either their thinking or their actions. But Jesus' gnostic followers had recognized oneness and had awakened to the Self. They were releasing the false mind and reconnecting with the One Mind of the Divine that allowed them to see everything in a new way. They were learning to be love, and live from the foundation of love and oneness rather than separation and specialness. They had no interest in following rules because their eyes had been opened to that fact that rules are man-made, not dictated by the Divine. They had experienced the truth of Jesus' words and they were free from the concepts of sin and obedience.

Those who reach understanding through gnosis are dead to the false mind's thought system and are resurrected to their true identity. The gnostic *Gospel of Philip* tells us, "Those who say they will die first and then rise are in error" because we should "receive the resurrection while alive." The gnostic writing, *The Treatise on Resurrection,* equates human 'life' with spiritual death and points out, "The world is an illusion! The resurrection is the revelation of what is, and the transformation of things, and transition into newness." Having been resurrected in awareness, Jesus' gnostic disciples no longer saw the world's laws as something that applied to them. This doesn't mean they were going to run out and break rules with abandon, but they would weigh rules in light of love and decide what fit with love and what didn't. This is why Jesus willingly and regularly ignored Jewish religious laws. For example, love told him it was more important to show love and heal on the Sabbath than keep the Sabbath laws.

We've learned that our universe *is* Divine Reality, but also contains a dream-like virtual reality that we project. As Jesus said, we can't successfully mount two horses or bend two bows, but that is exactly what each of us is trying to do when we project a body. Like a rider trying to mount two horses, we remain the Self but are trying to be the self. And we are succeeding at each about as well as an archer trying to hit a target using two bows and two arrows at the same time. Instead of at least one of the arrows hitting the target, they will no doubt both go far off course. And that is the case for us, our determination to live in conflict means we are not succeeding as either the Self or the self. *Everything* in our universe results from conscious thought. We truly are part of Divine consciousness, but we're still trying to serve the tiny part of consciousness that thinks it's a body and personality. Above all else, the verses and the parable about two masters in *Thomas* highlight the problem of a conflicted mind.

Focus isn't mathematical; it can't be divided and doled out evenly. Instead, we become unfocused and scattered. As a result, each thing we want to focus on suffers. This conflict is what Jesus was referring to when he said, "Whoever has something in hand will be given more, and whoever has nothing will be deprived of even the little that person has." When we remain in conflict, we think we have two things, but we really don't have either of them. Nothing can be 'added' because there is nothing there. When we resolve the conflict and make a choice, we do have something, and more can be added. When we close ourselves off from the One Mind by clinging to preconceived notions, attachments and aversions, our understanding shrivels into nothingness and all we're left with is the pseudo wisdom of the world. When we reconnect to the One Mind, there's no limit to the understanding we can receive. It just takes a little willingness to open the floodgates of knowing.

As Jesus pointed out, "a servant cannot serve two masters, or that servant will honor the one and offend the other." We are not slaves of God as some would claim, nor does the Divine want us to be. However, we are depriving ourselves and the Divine of the companionship and love we were created to share. But we can, and do, make ourselves *slaves to our own thoughts*. When we think from the false mind we become a slave to its perpetual desires and demands. And those desires keep us locked into a cycle of birth, death and misery we could easily avoid. The question is, do we want to continue allowing the self to be our master, or will we claim mastery by waking to Self.

As Jesus said so well, when we wake up we become something new that no longer fits with something old. A transformation takes place, and like new wine in old wineskins, this illusion can no longer contain the expansive Self, nor would we want it to. Our dualistic thought system is an experiment, a challenge that we can make a world of separation and specialness that's as successful as oneness. Our experiment has never been successful, and as Jesus pointed out, "A grapevine has been planted away from the Father. Since it was not strong, it will be pulled up by its root and will perish." But instead of Source pulling up this weak plant for us, it's up to each of us to recognize the problem and uproot it ourselves. The masters we must choose between are not God and Riches, but the two minds that are responsible for our thoughts. Again, the most important question we can ask ourselves is whether we want to continue allowing the self to be our master, or will we claim mastery by waking to Self. As always, the choice is ours.

Two Masters

Chapter Ten

What No Eye Has Seen

After looking at the quantum connections in the *Gospel of Thomas*, it should be little surprise that Jesus said, "I shall give you what no eye has seen, what no ear has heard, what no hand has touched, what has not arisen in the human heart." The senses long for what they can hear, taste, smell, see or touch and the brain desires what it can imagine. But it's obvious from what Jesus said that neither the brain nor the senses are able to take us where he went. We've learned that it takes a shift of consciousness, from the false mind/self that exists in isolation to True Mind/Self we share with All That Is.

The Frog in the Well

The Taoist master Chuang Tzu likened the false mind to a frog in a well. Secluded in its tiny habitat, it lives out its life completely unaware of the world outside. If another frog came to the edge of the well and tried to describe the ocean to the well frog, it would be unable to comprehend what was being said. The vastness, the sandy beaches, glorious sunsets and the creatures that dwell there would be more than it could imagine. The same is true for us. How could the brain or senses possibly come up with an accurate picture of quantum reality? And yet, we can have an ongoing, personal experience of the Divine when we connect with the One Mind because the brain and senses are *not* involved.

Many feel that they have a relationship with God, but it's indirect. They may read and quote scriptures, pray, attend church and do good works, however, this falls far short of what Jesus was talking about. When we begin thinking with the One Mind, we have the privilege of direct access to the Source and repository of all wisdom. We won't have to hunt for it or beg for it, but just be willing to listen and accept it. Then we will live as Rumi recommended when he said, "Listen, and your whole life will become a conversation in thought and act between you and Him, directly, wordlessly, now and always. It was to enjoy this conversation that you and I were created." Rumi's words lead us to one of the most interesting statements Jesus made in *Thomas*:

Jesus said, "Let one who seeks not stop seeking until one finds. When one finds, one will be troubled. When one is troubled, one will marvel and will reign over all."

The Greek version contains some subtle differences:

Let one who seeks not stop seeking until one finds. When one finds, one will be astonished, and having been astonished one will reign, and having reigned, one will rest.

Jesus' short statement is probably the most succinct, and accurate, report on spiritual awakening ever written. Jesus understood through first-hand experience that *the details of each person's journey are different*, but he also knew that spiritual awakening usually includes the six more generalized items that are mentioned: seeking, finding, being troubled, being astonished, reigning and resting.

Seek Until You Find

Before anything happens, something has to trigger the journey. We can think of this as the first awakenings from a dream. We would all prefer to have pleasant dreams and wake up gradually, slowly readjusting ourselves to our wakened state. This happens when we've taken our time to assess life and gradually come to the conclusion that's something's missing. This is often felt as a disconnect with the world that's often described as feeling like an alien being that doesn't belong here. Or it can manifest as a discontent, restlessness or emptiness that can no longer be satisfied by anything the material world has to offer. Some of us wake up when life has become so untenable we've hit bottom and don't see anywhere else to go.

A few wake up abruptly and are shocked into sudden awareness. Although this sort of 'wake up call' appears to be very exciting, the drama quickly fades. Awareness that's reached so rapidly still has to be assimilated, which also requires a spiritual journey. So, we can start at the beginning and travel to the end, or we can start at the end and have to backtrack until we find the beginning. Either way, seeking will take place.

Seeking as a Journey

We're using the terms 'seeking' and 'journey' because of their common association with spiritual awakening, but frankly, they're both quite misleading. The seeker really isn't going anywhere outside themselves and the journey is not really about getting from one place to another. What is being sought is already our possession, but the false mind has buried it so deeply, few of us know it's there.

If we're going to use the journey metaphor, we might imagine the pioneers who crossed America in a Conestoga wagon. At the beginning of the trip, the wagons were crammed with everything the pioneers valued and wanted to carry with them into their new life. But historians tell us the trails to the west were littered with items the pioneers soon regarded as unnecessary burdens. By the time they reached their destination, they had let go of everything that had been important for the life they had once led, but now held little value. As they began to see things from the perspective of a new and very different life, their value system underwent a radical change. When they arrived at their destination, not only was the wagon far lighter, they had been changed by the process.

Seeking as Excavation

The seeker can also be thought of as an archeologist excavating a dig. As we painstakingly remove layers of debris, we sift and sort, separating the valuable from the valueless. And like the archeologist, we usually find a monumental pile of worthless trash that was hiding a precious treasure. Seeking is important not because it gets you to a destination, but its value lies in the digging, sifting, weighing process that's taking place. It's a simple process, but it can be, like any excavation, messy, tiring and frustrating as we root through our social conditioning and the dualistic thinking of the false mind.

Sometimes we dig through misperceptions like soft sand that keeps caving back in on itself; just when we think we're there, the false mind reburies us in the same old worthless thoughts and fears. Other times we spend what seems like an endless amount of time carefully scraping away minute bits of rock hard misperceptions and feel as if we'll never get through the process. Or we dig through what we believe is the final layer just to find several more we hadn't been aware of.

While we're excavating it's good to remember that we were the ones who mired the treasure under piles of debris. The process of letting go is easy or difficult depending on how much dirt the false mind has piled over the treasure, and how attached we are to it. *This is not a test from the Divine, it's completely self-inflicted.* Like the pioneers, we're the ones who packed the wagon and we're the ones who have to decide just how important each item is as we try to get the wagon through another mountain pass.

How do we decide between what's worth hanging on to and what should be thrown out of the wagon? If you were training to be an archeologist, you wouldn't be included on a dig until you had learned the jargon that's particular to the field. Otherwise, you might misunderstand the directions you were being given and ignore something of importance. The same is true as we peel away the layers of the false mind. The Divine, the true Self that we're seeking, speaks the language of the heart, of love, and of oneness. That language is intuitive and comes to us through heart intelligence that bypasses the false mind and the brain's logic. As Rumi pointed out, "In every moment, in every event of your life, the Beloved is whispering to you exactly what you need to hear and know." But we won't hear it until we quiet the false mind's incessant babbling and welcome the voice of the Self.

Since we chose duality over oneness, we gave the false mind free reign to rant and rage whether we like what we're hearing or not, but the voice of the Divine won't interfere with freewill and requires an invitation before it can be heard. The more we involve the false mind and the brain's logic in the excavation and evaluation process, the more difficult it will be. The false mind is like a packrat. As soon as something is put on the 'throw' pile, it will drag it back to the 'keep' pile. Since the brain also wants to keep the status quo, the process can feel endless.

Fortunately, as we willingly replace thoughts of separation with thoughts of oneness, we're inviting the Divine in and turning up the volume. And turning 'up' the volume of the Divine means simultaneously turning 'down' the volume on the false mind/brain. Two things accomplished with one turn of the knob! Since the false mind can only exist on dualistic thoughts, this has the double advantage of allowing us to do our sorting more easily and weakens the hold the false mind has enjoyed. This also becomes easier as we realize that the things we let go of didn't really have the meaning we thought they had, and the things we're replacing them with are changing us in ways that we could not have imagined.

The excavation process also reveals unexpected gems, such as mystical experiences or deep insights that seem to come from nowhere. These gems can be reassuring, enthralling and yet deceiving if we mistake them for the goal. Some seekers become so engrossed in the experience, they become like a drug addict constantly trying to replicate the first high. These experiences can't be forced and they're *not* necessary to our process. As Jesus said, "Let him who seeks *continue* seeking until he finds," and "Let one who seeks *not stop seeking* until one finds." But how do we know when we've actually "found?" [italics ours]

As we said earlier, Jesus' admonition to not stop seeking until we find implies both self-responsibility and effort. However the effort is not involved in learning, but in unlearning. Like a pearl hidden inside a shell, its beauty cannot be appreciated until the covering is removed. But unlike the shell of a pearl that can be separated from the pearl very quickly, the densely layered thought system of the false self covers the Self with veil after veil of perception, social conditioning, attachments and aversions.

The 'self' That Isn't There

When we've removed the veils and find the Self, we also discover the false mind's most jealously guarded secret: it doesn't actually exist. It is not an entity, but the result of smoke and mirrors. The cause of the self is a thought system based on polarized duality. The effect is a portion of the mind that can hold that concept. Reverse the process, peel away the layers of thought that sustain it and it is no longer there. Since the self is 'disposable' it also means that when we allowed it to come into existence, we also wanted a way out and included that in the plan. Sadly, most of have forgotten about this escape route.

Like all thought systems, the false mind continually perpetuates its own flawed beliefs and values. First and foremost, it's dedicated to keeping us focused on separation and specialness. It's aided in this endeavor by the brain and the body, not because they are aware and plotting against the Self, but because of their own natural inclinations. The brain is a survival mechanism, for that reason it's happiest when keeping the status quo and agitated when it's confronted with change. Stripping away the thought system it's accustomed to will initially make the brain quite uncomfortable and it will do its best to draw our attention back to the rut it felt safe with.

The body simply wants to be given whatever it craves. We all know the body will reward us with sensations of pleasure once its requests are met, but the pleasure is short lived and a new request is quickly made. We spend a good deal of time each day taking care of those requests. Many of them are benign, such as putting a jacket on when the body is cold, but a large percentage can become addictive and cause the body to sabotage itself.

Whenever we think or do something repeatedly, the brain and body set up a complex group of physiological reactions that send a chemical cocktail through the system. Although these natural chemicals are made by the body itself, they're still addictive. As we continue to repeat a thought or behavior, we get more dependent on the chemical 'hit' that comes with it. At that point, changing the thought or behavior means we have to go without the 'hit' until a new neural pathway is constructed. This process can make us very uncomfortable, as anyone who has tried to break a habit has found out. The false mind is happy to let the brain and body run rampant, but if we persist in releasing thoughts and behaviors we no longer find valuable, the Self will take control of both. The Self is aware of when the brain is needed to reason and analyze and when to indulge the body, but it no longer lets them run the show.

It would seem as we peel away the veils that the false mind is doing its best to appropriate the spiritual path. Actually it's just busy trying to figure out how it can adapt the new information we're taking in to fit it's thought system. When we look at the spiritual situation in the world, it quickly becomes obvious that it's been extremely successful. Alan Watts accurately described the problem when he said, "In practicing spiritual disciplines as well as in trying to acquire faith, most of us are like monkeys. We do not understand the saint's inner state, and we are trying to attain it by the mere mimicry of its outward signs."

Religion often tells us that if we read Jesus' words, go through rituals, say prayers and try to behave like Jesus, we will be a Christian. That's accurate, it will turn us into a follower of Christ, but it will never turn us into a Christ. But Jesus, like every other spiritual master, rejected the idea of followers and encouraged everyone who heard him to become his 'twin.' As Watts goes on to say, "It avails nothing to ape the exterior actions or even the interior ideas of [an inspired person] unless we understand the meaning which these ideas and actions express…our efforts to be like the great ones are so many attempts to produce the cause by the effect, to make the tail wag the dog." This takes us full circle to the beginning of *Thomas* where Jesus told his followers it would be the ones that discover "the interpretation of these sayings" who "will not taste death." That discovery cannot come from anyone or anything outside us, it can only take place within.

Finding

When an archeologist sets out on a dig they usually have an expectation, a hope or a general idea of what they might find, but few of them know beforehand exactly what will be hiding under the rubble. Sometimes what is discovered was expected, other times it's a complete surprise. This type of 'finding' is a paradox that mirrors spiritual seeking and finding. We have a general idea what we're looking for, but it's impossible for us to know exactly what it will look like when we find it. Sometimes what we discover fits with our expectations, but often, we're confronted with something we had never imagined.

As mentioned before, there can be several points during the excavating process when we feel that we've reached the goal only to find much later that there's more digging to do. This may happen when we need time to assimilate new information and the changes we're making. Or, at times it can be the false mind getting involved and convincing us we're 'there' in an attempt to stop further progress. Regardless, there will still be questions and doubts that let us know we have further to go. If that's the case, how can we feel certain when we've reached the point of 'finding?'

How do you know when you've solved a puzzle? Jesus gave two important clues. The first is "seek until you find." Imagine a jigsaw puzzle with hundreds of pieces, but you don't have the box so you have no picture to guide you. When you've put enough pieces together that there's no doubt in your mind what the entire picture is, you're there, and the puzzle is solved. That doesn't mean that you can't still put in a few pieces; those pieces may add a little detail, but they won't really alter your understanding of the picture. When Jesus said not to stop seeking until you find, he was telling us that there is a place where the picture is clear and the seeking stops. We will continue to add details until we return to oneness, but we will understand the 'big picture.' The second clue lies in the words, "When one finds, one will be troubled."

Being Troubled

We might also substitute words like shocked, stunned or even distressed. Although Jesus said we would be troubled when we find, we can also feel troubled as we seek. This is not because what we discover is actually troubling, but because it's usually not at all what we expected to find. It's shocking to find out that nothing is as we thought it was; that the proverbial rug has been pulled out from under us.

It helps to understand that our social conditioning and the dualistic thoughts of the false mind couldn't possibly prepare us for reality. As the Taoist master Chuang-Tzu astutely observed, "It's impossible to explain the ocean to a frog in a well." When we begin seeking, we are that frog. We begin with the certainty of our social conditioning. We're so sure this world is real and we are the body and personality, we don't even think to question it. When we begin to understand what is real and what isn't and discover the material universe is an ephemeral manifestation of an infinite reality, it's bound to trouble us. Just as the ocean is far beyond the comprehension of the frog in the well, we can't begin to understand reality until we've climbed far enough out of the well of virtual reality to get a glimpse of it.

It's exciting to read about quantum research, to discover that this world of matter is not reality. And it's mind-blowing to hear that we live in a fully conscious universe. But it can be quite troubling to try to digest the full import of the fact that you yourself are non-local consciousness, a part of everything in existence. The brain, formerly so assured of its own supremacy, reels as it tries to assimilate the information. And, since most of us have been taught that God exists outside the universe, it can be troubling to cope with the thought that the Divine permeates everything in existence, and we are all That.

We may also be troubled or fearful at the loss of the self. The false mind has convinced us that we *are* the body and the personality; awakening demonstrates that this is not the case. But we've spent a lifetime building, supporting and defending the personality, and we've been taught that our life begins and ends with this body. We fear that without our "story" we'll lose our individuality and eventually become lost in oneness. Or we may have heard that there's a "void" of nothingness at the end of the spiritual journey. This sounds so frightening it stops many seekers cold, but as we've learned, it isn't true.

The Divine *is* reality, and reality includes everything that exists and the potential for everything that can ever exist, not the opposite. In *The Crest Jewel of Discrimination*, Shankara explained to a student that the void is what's left after the false mind is no longer deceiving us, but there is still an observer, a conscious being, aware of the oneness that remains after the thought of duality is gone. If there truly was an empty void we all merged into, there would be no consciousness left to be aware.

We don't lose ourselves in oneness, but rather experience the truth of who we actually are. And as Jesus said, this truth does set us free. Truth is always liberating, it's the false mind that imprisons and limits us. We live in a universe of consciousness and potential, which informs us that we also live in a universe of free will and infinite creativity. Oneness means equality, not sameness. In reality, every child of Source has the same talents but the infinite creative diversity that's apparent in the material universe demonstrates that each one expresses their talents differently.

Spiritual masters agree that the defining characteristic of Divine Presence is love, and we came into existence to give and receive that love. Obviously, love can only be appreciated, exchanged and expressed between beings that can choose for themselves and exercise free will. We give up the personality shaped by the dualistic thinking of the false mind, but that doesn't mean the Self is without personality. The difference is that the personality of Self would shine as a facet of the universal diamond rather than trying to be the entire gem.

Letting Go

As we transition from the self to the Self, at some point we will need to release our attachment to the body and personality we're currently projecting. It's something we'll want to do, but fear to do at the same time. We're feeling a pull in both directions, to let go and hang on. And, for a short while we may feel as if we're hanging in midair without a net. Rumi compares this moment of transition to a man who takes an arduous journey to see a great lion. When he finally gets within sight of the lion, he becomes fearful and can't go any closer. Someone reminds him that his love for the lion has brought him this far. If he will just go to the lion and tenderly stroke him, the lion will return his love. Like the man in the journey, we may feel that every step up this point was easy, but once we approach the lion directly, there is no turning back. Rumi tells us these last few steps are the only real steps on our journey.

This transition signals the false mind's loss of control, and it never gives up easily. It will try to make us feel as if we're facing a lion, but the false mind has never been truthful. It can fling baseless thoughts and emotions at us, but it has no power. Everyone willing to pass through this "troubled" feeling and approach the lion in love will do so unscathed, and astonished.

Being Astonished

As the seeker peels away the layers, Jesus warns us that we will be 'astonished' by what we experience. The level of astonishment Jesus was speaking about is not going to come simply from listening to his words. We all know that reading someone's second-hand account of a sporting event and attending it cannot be compared. There is a far greater chasm between reading second-hand words *about* God and personally experiencing the Divine! If you aren't astonished, you haven't had the experience yet.

Even when we're limited by our brain and senses, the universe is so amazing; we can be left in a state of awe and astonishment whenever we contemplate it. But the astonishment that Jesus was speaking of goes so much further than intellectual observations could ever take us. He was speaking of the profound astonishment which results from gnosis, the direct, personal experience of the Divine. Gnosis couldn't possibly reveal All That Is in total, but it gives each of us exactly the glimpse of Reality that will be most meaningful to us. The core feeling of overwhelming oneness and love remains the same, but the details are tailored to reach individual hearts.

When the Taoist master Lao-Tzu said, "The Tao that can be spoken of is not the Tao," he was not only referring to the failure of language to express the experience, but the impossibility of conveying to another person what touched us personally. This is also another place where 'holy' writings fail us. As Shankara noted, "Study of the scriptures is fruitless as long as [Ultimate Reality] has not been experienced. And when [Ultimate Reality] has been experienced, it is useless to read the scriptures." Language cannot convey the jaw-dropping astonishment of gnosis, but we can glimpse the results that are exhibited in the life of the experiencer.

Jesus was born into an extremely legalistic society where every action was ruled by a rigid code that exposed people's shortcomings and condemned them as sinners on a daily basis. Instead of leading to love, the laws encouraged judgment, and judgment led to condemnation, hatred and vengeance. When Jesus experienced the Divine it turned his life and his value system upside down. Instead of experiencing a God of judgment he saw and felt something entirely different: absolute, irresistible, infinite, unconditional love and the oneness of All That Is. This experience so overwhelmed him, it informed everything he did and said for the rest of that lifetime, and it carried him back to oneness when he let go of the body. Jesus' astonishment shocked his followers when he encouraged them to stop judging, pray for their enemies and see everyone as their neighbor. Imagine how difficult it was for them to comprehend his assertion that the law they lived by would be unnecessary if they lived in love!

The majority of Jesus' followers remained asleep and never got to the point of finding or being troubled or astonished. When we do find, it's mind-boggling to realize that we have been sleepwalking through one dream after another in the valueless pursuit of separation and specialness. This may make us feel ashamed or stupid, but there's no need to feel that way. The Divine has given us free will and a safe opportunity to explore. The *Gospel of Truth* assures us, "The Father's Word goes out in the

All as the fruition of his heart and expression of his will. It supports all and chooses all."

Once we've experienced the universe as it actually is, we have the advantage of understanding both the virtual reality of separation and the quantum reality of oneness. We can navigate both with the peaceful assurance that there is nothing to fear. When we recognize the experience of the Divine *is* our reality and allow it to permeate us, *we become the experience*, not a mere observer. Like Jesus, we'll live in a state of astonishment and serve as a living mirror that reflects the Divine. And as the Greek version of *Thomas* adds, no matter how troubled or astonished we may feel, we cannot help but marvel, and then Jesus assures us we will reign!

Reigning

But what will we reign over? We can tease out the meaning of Jesus' words by looking at a statement he made in John 16:33, "In the world you have tribulation: but be of good cheer; I have conquered the world." This quote is usually taken to mean that Jesus conquered the world on our behalf. We're going to look at some reasons to understand his words in a more proactive way; because he conquered and reigned, we can too.

Reigning and ruling imply the power and authority to dictate and enforce laws that others must obey. And the word conqueror usually brings to mind someone like Genghis Khan, Julius Caesar or Alexander the Great who used force to overpower and subjugate. From a spiritual standpoint, those who have ruled, reigned and conquered in this world have accomplished nothing of value. In the end, the false mind conquered all of them, just as it does any of us who continue to desire separation and specialness.

Although there are many verses in the New Testament gospels that support the gnostic view, most Christian religions focus on the verses that support the messianic/apocalyptic view. As a result, most Christians believe all Jesus' early followers expected him to be a conqueror in the most forceful sense of the word. Certainly many Jews wanted a warrior messiah who would literally vanquish their Roman oppressors. Jesus' messianic followers must have felt crushed and confused when shortly after saying he had conquered the world,

Jesus was killed by the oppressors they expected him to defeat.

From a political perspective, Jesus' words make no sense; from a spiritual standpoint, they make perfect sense. He had rejected the thought system that projects the illusion of separation. He had conquered the false self and was thinking with the One Mind. When he spoke those words, he had transcended everything that had kept him from his true identity except the body. Like every spiritual master, he realized that the only world he could conquer and reign over is the one created by the false self.

The Coptic version, adds reign 'over all,' giving the impression that reigning meant having authority over others. But this addition can also be understood from a different perspective. When we think about it, we realize that misunderstanding the universe and our place in it is the foundation of all the fear and misery in our world. When we understand who we really are, we know nothing can harm us. When we're thinking from the One Mind, we lose our fear and without fear, no one can frighten us or reign over us. Our liberation allows us to 'reign over all' in the sense that no one has any real power over us. This was certainly the case with Jesus. The Romans believed they had the power to bring Jesus' life to an end, but that was only because they didn't understand what life really is. In the gnostic *Gospel of Peter* Jesus tells a very different story of the crucifixion when he says:

> *The one you see smiling and laughing above the cross is the living Jesus. The one into whose hands and feet they are driving nails is his fleshly part, the substitute for him. They are putting to shame the one who came into being in the likeness of the living Jesus. Look at him and look at me.*

The false mind is certain the body must be protected at all costs, but Jesus proved that even the most appalling treatment of the body can't affect our true Self. Remember Jesus promised that the ones who discovered the interpretation of his sayings would "not taste death." The quantum paradigm tells us that Jesus was correct. Only a God that exists outside the universe could make mortal creatures, giving and taking life as if it were a game. But the children of an immortal Source who creates out of Self must also be immortal since the Source cannot, and will not, destroy

Self. The supposed 'death' of the body is a transition. The consciousness that projected it can sleep and dream, but it can never die.

Although Jesus' gnostic followers understood there was no reason for Jesus to die a sacrificial death, they appreciated the fact that when circumstances brought him to suffering, he used the opportunity to show in an undeniable manner that all suffering is an illusion. Yes, the body feels pain and it resists its demise, but only because we have done such an excellent job of persuading it that it is far more than it actually is. Jesus understood the body was a substitute he had projected. He was ready and willing to let the body go and wake up fully in oneness, so the 'death' of the body gave him the ultimate opportunity to reign over all who thought they were conquering him.

Even in the body, those who have awakened and understand their true nature reign over all since they no longer fear. Fear that we are this body and our life ends with its demise causes people to give themselves over to all kinds of physical, emotional and spiritual slavery. When you know that no one can touch your true Self or cause you any real harm, you reign. Although many involved in religion seek to reign over others and exert power in the world, gnostic Christians understood that they reigned through knowledge. When we live as the Self, the thought of wielding power over anyone or anything becomes abhorrent. Power in oneness is as ridiculous as the concept of ownership.

And Then Rest

The Greek version of *Thomas* adds the additional fascinating tidbit of information: "...and having reigned, one will rest." After waking to the Self, we can still continue to project a body and act out the drama of separation for as long as we wish. But once awakened, we play the game from an entirely different perspective. Like a person who stands on a mountain top and surveys the world around them, we see what those in the valley cannot possibly imagine.

The ability to understand both the virtual and the real allows us to remain connected to oneness and still participate in the world, but we do so from the position of a detached observer. Virtual reality becomes a game that we know we've already won but still may continue playing. As long as we choose to continue to project virtual reality it will be impossible to escape the dualistic thought system that keeps it in turmoil. However, we can find rest within our own peacefulness despite the chaos that swirls around us. But true rest comes when we're ready to let go of our projections and literally return to oneness. Let's find out by considering one more of Jesus' parables:

> *Jesus said, "Look, the sower went out, took a handful of seeds, and scattered them. Some fell on the road, and birds came and pecked them up. Others fell on the rock, and they did not take root in the soil and did not produce heads of grain. Others fell on thorns, and they choked the seed and worms devoured them. And others fell on good soil, and it brought forth a good crop."*

The point to the parable is found a few verses later when Jesus says, "When the crop ripened, the person came quickly with sickle in hand and harvested it. Whoever has ears to hear should hear."

Be Ripe For the Harvest

Rumi tells us, "…in every event of your life, the Beloved is whispering to you exactly what you need to hear and know." These whispers are like the seeds in Jesus' parable. But as the parable demonstrates, no one is forced to listen to their inner voice or allow the seeds of truth to grow. These seeds can grow only in the fertile soil of the heart, but as Jesus' parable explains, many of them are rejected and fall in places where they wither and die. This is not surprising when we see how the false mind keeps us busy and focused on meaningless drama. Some of the seeds do take root, but they're not nurtured, and are easily choked out by the cares of the day before they can become strong enough to rise above the weeds. And still others are eaten away by the worms of fear.

But some take Rumi's advice and "Be crumbled ground so wildflowers will come up where you are." If the heart is willing, we will listen to the whisperings of Source and the seeds will grow strong. Unlike the Bible where weeds are burned and destroyed, this harvester takes only the crop that has reached maturity and leaves everything else as it is. Of course the sower/harvester in this parable is Source, and as soon as the crop is ready, the ripened fruit is gathered.

The point of all sowing is the harvest. The farmer's efforts would go unrewarded if the field was not harvested. Although spiritual masters have always pointed to this harvest as the result the Divine longs for, the false mind would like to convince us there is something better. Currently, many teachers claim that consciousness is evolving and a new age of spiritual understanding is dawning. While we feel certain these teachers have only the best intentions in mind, they've forgotten that spiritual awakening is an *unlearning* process, one that eliminates valueless thoughts. To say consciousness was evolving would mean Source is a product of evolution that was continually subject to change. Other teachers claim that it is God's will that humanity evolve into a higher life form able to create a utopian world that supports all life. This view denies our true identity and would keep us locked in a continuous cycle of birth and death rather than a return to Reality.

Although Jesus said the Farmer came quickly to harvest the crop, he didn't rush the harvest. Like all farmers, the Divine waits until the crop is at the peak of its readiness. This means that the harvest is never against our will; no one returns to oneness until it is their only desire. At that point, the greatest treasures this world has to offer seem like meaningless trinkets next to Reality. When we're ready to wake up fully in oneness we do so because there is nothing left of the false mind or its ability to project another useless dream. We're ready to rest from duality and give up the pursuit of specialness. This is the Supreme Goal that all masters, including Jesus, have pointed to. Jesus gives us one more parable about children that directs us to this goal:

> *Mary said to Jesus, "What are your disciples like?" He said, "They are like children living in a field that is not theirs. When the owners of the field come, they will say, "give our field back to us." They take off their clothes in front of them in order to give it back to them, and they return their field to them."*

Since you've already discovered the meaning of many of the symbols Jesus used, this verse may not seem so cryptic. We understand the children are actually spiritual masters. They have let go of the false self and are thinking from the One Mind. As you now know, their clothing is the body. In this case, the field is the illusionary world of separation that's been constructed by the false self. We own the field when we think with the false mind (or rather the field owns us), but these 'children' no longer have any desire to claim ownership. Since the 'children' are now completely aware of the illusion, those who still cling to it can't tolerate their presence and demand that they hand it back and leave. Since the children have given up their attachment to the field and all it stands for, they readily let go of the body, return to oneness and leave the field in the hands of those who still claim ownership of it.

The Mundaka Upanishad echoes the teaching of Jesus found in the *Gospel of Thomas* when it says:

> *Self is everywhere, shining forth from all beings, vaster than the vast, subtler than the most subtle, unreachable, yet nearer than breath, than heartbeat. Ear cannot hear it nor tongue utter it. Only in deep absorption can the mind, grown pure and silent, merge with the formless truth. He who finds it is free; he has found himself; he has solved the great riddle; his heart is forever at peace. Whole, he enters into the Whole. His personal Self returns to its*

radiant, intimate, deathless Source. As rivers lose name and form when they disappear into the sea, the sage leaves behind all traces when he disappears into the light. *Perceiving the truth, he becomes that truth; he passes beyond all suffering, beyond earth; all the knots of his heart are loosed.*

And Rumi reminds us, "The second you stepped into this world of existence a ladder was placed before you to help you escape. When you pass beyond this human form...plunge into the vast ocean of consciousness."

What No Eye Has Seen

Afterword

After looking at the quantum connections in the *Gospel of Thomas*, it should be little surprise that Jesus said, "I shall give you what no eye has seen, what no ear has heard, what no hand has touched, what has not arisen in the human heart."

Jesus was no different from any of us, but through gnosis he experienced the Divine. It's clear that the *Gospel of Thomas* is his invitation to trade perception for vision and experience the truth behind illusion. That 'knowing' is available to each and every one of us. This short book has focused on the verses in the *Gospel of Thomas* that most clearly display the result of Jesus' direct, personal experience of the Divine and the understanding of the universe that resulted from it. But there are many more gems waiting for your discovery.

The Jesus that we've come to know would be appalled to think his words had become an object of belief that kept others from the direct experience of Source. For Jesus' gnostic followers, words were no more than a jumping off point for their own exploration. In the same way, the discoveries of quantum physics are just another way for us to start thinking more deeply about Reality. Jesus' words were meant to inspire his listeners to start their own quest, not limit them. Faith and trust can only arise out of the foundation of our own experiences, not someone else's.

If you profess belief in the words we've written and stop there, we've failed you. Our desire is that the synergy of science and spirituality in *Thomas* will open a door of possibility that supports and encourages your own personal inquiry. As you discard the blinders put on by the false mind, you will see that the Divine is whispering to you from a thousand sources. Follow the advice of Rumi and "make everything in you an ear, each atom of your being, and you will hear at every moment what the Source is whispering to you , just to you and for you...exactly what you need to hear and know."

Afterword

Index

Numbers

1Timothy, book of 134
3D 45

A

Adam and Eve 100, 117
All That Is 46, 59
angels 102
apocalyptic 15, 67
Aquinas, Saint Thomas 16, 144
Armageddon 69
atonement 22
attachment 185
attachments 143
austerity 136
aversions 143
awareness 48

B

being astonished 172
being troubled 167
belief 189
Bible 118, 123, 182
Bible scholars 34
Big Bang 51, 52
biophotons 127
birth of the body 102
body 44, 92, 115, 129, 169
body, as a constraint 103
body, mortal 101
Bohm, David 45
Book of Thomas 76

brain 30, 44, 91, 120
brain, as obedient to the heart 139
brain, as survival mechanism 163
Buddha 93

C

camel 135
catholic, definiton 34
children 184
choice 55, 117
Christ 19
Christian writings, early 23
Christians, early 33
Christians, gnostic 47, 180
Chuang Tzu 153, 168
church, institutionalized 22, 73, 100
circumcision 81
clergy class 33
clothing, as symbol for body 103
competition 57
condemnation 83, 173
conqueror 176
conscious oneness 43
consciousness 29, 115, 116, 117, 118
consciousness, altered 29
consciousness, as immortal 72, 179
consciousness, at subatomic level 42
consciousness, outside the body 45
consciousness, shift in 153
consequences 22
Coptic, definition 70
cosmological constant 53
create 118
Creation of the World and the Alien Man 126
creations 118
creativity 117, 170
Crest Jewel of Discrimination, The 169
crucifixion 178

cycle of birth and death 149
cyclical 71

D

darkness 123
death 20, 23, 178
death, as illuison 129
death, sacrificial 179
demi-god 22, 74
desires of the heart 139
determinists 55
Dialogue of the Savior 30, 37, 108, 128
diet, dietary laws 82
disciples 32
Divine consciousness 148
Divine Ground 28
Divine Light 124
Divine light 128
Divine love 144
Divine Reality 147
doctrine 31
dogma 31
dream 47, 57
drunk 106
dualistic belief system 38
dualistic thinking 158
duality 56, 105, 123, 137, 160

E

Eastern philosophy 43, 54, 115
ego 59
Einstein, Albert 16
emotions 91
energy 71, 112, 116, 118
energy potential 117
equality 170
euaggelion 32
evil 123

evolution 50
evolution, spiritual 183
experiential 27

F

Faith 190
False Mind 59
false mind 86, 105, 142, 146, 153, 162
false self 82, 89, 177
fast 82, 145
fast from the world 87
fasting 146
fear 179, 182
field 184
finding 165
forgetfulness, willful 22
forgiveness 21
free will 55, 56, 117, 140, 142, 170
frog in a well 153
Fuller, Buckminster 99

G

Genesis 100, 117
gentiles 33
gnosis 27, 30, 35, 47, 146, 172, 173, 189
gnostic 23, 24, 31
gnostic followers, Jesus' 34
Gnostic gospels 27
gnostic gospels 14
Gnosticism 30
goal, spiritual 161
God and riches 133, 150
God incarnate 19, 22
Godhead, triune 22, 73
God's image 100
God's kingdom, see kingdom, God's
good and evil 123
good works 154

goodness, original 21
gospel 32
Gospel of Mary 21, 137
Gospel of Peter 178
Gospel of Philip 130, 146
Gospel of Truth 20, 47, 174
Guth, Alan 52

H

Haggadah 126
harvest 181, 183
hatred 173
Hawking, Steven 52
healer 20
healing, physical 20
healing the mind 22
heart 139
Hebrews, book of 21, 134
heretic 23
higher mind 58
Hillman James 31
hologram 45
holographic film 112
holographic image 46
holographic universe 45
holy books 142, 143
humanity vs. divinity, Jesus' 22

I

identity, true 123
ignorance, as sin 22
illusion 44, 47, 147, 189
imagination 117
immortal 72
individuality 119
inflation, theory of 52
information 86
intelligence, life-giving 29

interference pattern 91, 113
Intuition 31
intuitive 31

J

Jefferson, Thomas 69
Jesus, as human 73, 97
Jesus, as liberator 81
Jesus, as living 71
Jesus' persona 22, 74
Jewish theocracy 69
Jews 33
John, book of 21, 33, 73, 175
John the Baptizer 145
journey, spiritual 155
Judaism 33
judgment 83, 173

K

kingdom 75
kingdom, a government 75
kingdom, as government 98
kingdom, God's 49, 87, 108, 135
kingdom, quantum 98
knowing 27

L

Lao Tzu 116, 173
law 137
law, a prison 82
law of love 144, 147
law, of Moses 81
lawgiver 137, 141
Laws of Nature 141
leader 81
legalism 83
legalistic 81

letting go 159, 171
liberation 82, 177
light 89, 94, 123
light and life 124
light, as connection with the Divine 130
light, as universal matrix 127
light, Divine 123, 126
light of the world 124
light, quantum 125
linear 71
lion 171
literalism 34
living Jesus 129
living water 77
local 115
love 23, 81, 144, 170
love, Divine 99
love, God as 54, 120
love, unconditional 81
Luke, book of 33, 66, 73, 100, 133

M

Mark, book of 33, 66, 73
mass 125
master 19, 81
master, spiritual 13, 28, 54, 93, 142, 165, 183
matter 42, 44, 71
Matthew, book of
   33, 66, 73, 85, 133, 134, 137, 145
messiah 19, 67, 74
mind 46
mind, conflicted 148
mistake 22
money 134
money, as root of evil 134
money, quantum view of 137
Monoimus 49
moral codes 99, 141

mortal 100
motivation, inner 136
mystery schools 35

N

Nag Hammadi 27, 65, 70
Nasadiya Sukta 55
nature 16
needle's eye 134
New Testament
    14, 21, 65, 73, 81, 85, 88, 100, 133, 136, 144, 145, 176
nightmare 47
non-local 112
non-local oneness 115, 120, 141
non-local reality 111
nothingness 119

O

obedience 82, 108, 136, 146
One Mind 58, 86, 129
One Mind of God 30
oneness
    56, 57, 98, 105, 118, 144, 146, 160, 170, 185
oneness, and choices 140
oneness, indivisible 99
opinion 24, 32
oral tradition 32
orthodox 23, 24, 34
outward appearance 136

P

pagan 74
parable 57, 65
parables 36
parameters, universal operating 99, 141, 142
paranormal 29
perception 86, 92, 104, 189

Perennial Philosophy 28
perfection 21
personal identity 119
personality 72, 92, 115, 129, 169
Peter 21
Peter group 33
Pharisees 85, 145
photon 112, 117
photons 111
physicists 111
physics, Classical, Newtonian 41
pleasure 163
polarized duality 57
potential 43, 112, 116
poverty 97
prayer 82, 154
preconceived notions 143
probability wave 112
prodigal son 57
projection 56
Psalms, book of 124
punishment 22, 118, 130

Q

Q 66, 73
quanta, definition 41
quantum, definition 41
quantum physics 15, 38, 41, 190
quantum physics, definition 41
quelle 66

R

Reality 117
regulations 136
reigning 175
religious codes 99
religious rules 141
rest 180

resurrection 19, 146
rich man 134
riches 133
ritual 31, 82
Roman Empire 33
Romans, book of 21
rules 31, 81, 136
rules, as unnecessary 144
Rumi
    55, 120, 128, 130, 154, 159, 171, 181, 182, 186, 190

S

Sabbath laws 147
sacrifice 22, 82, 108
salvation 23
sameness 119, 170
savior 14, 19, 67
sayings gospel 66
Sayings Gospel of Q 66
scarcity 56, 57
science 38
Secret Book of John, The 124
secular world 134
seeking 156
seeking as a journey 156
seeking as excavation 158
Self 61, 87, 107, 146, 147
self 60, 86, 107, 147
Self-awareness 89
self-determination 82
self-examination 82
self-help 32
self-improvement 89
self-responsibility 161
separate forms 56
separation 44, 56, 72, 88, 118, 130, 146, 174
separation, and choices 140
Sermon on the Mount 124

Shankara 169, 173
signs 37
Silvanus 30, 37
sin 19, 21, 23, 137, 146
sin, original 21
social conditioning 158, 167
Son of God, only begotten 19, 22
son of man 75
soul 61, 101
specialness 56, 57, 72, 88, 118, 130, 146, 174
spirit creature 100
spiritual awakening 87, 156, 183
spiritual master, see master, spiritual
spiritual nourishment 88
status quo 160
subatomic particles 42
suffering 56
suffering, as illusion 129
suffering, Jesus' 129
Supreme Goal 184
symbolic language 35, 101
Symbols 36

T

teacher 20, 77
teacher, wisdom 23
The Hymn of the Pearl 47
Theodosius 22, 73
Thomas, as twin 70
Treatise on Resurrection 146
trinity doctrine 22, 74
true identity 22, 144
true mind 58
True Mind/Self 153
true Self 61
trust 190
truth 21, 22, 189
twin 76

two masters 136
two masters in Thomas 144

U

unconditional love 174
universal mind 30
universe, definition 99
unlearning 183
Upanishads 43, 49, 61, 114, 124, 138, 185

V

Valentinus 55, 120
valuable and valueless 158
vengeance 173
virtual reality 45, 56, 59, 104, 137
vision 92, 104, 189
void 115, 169
void, as all potential 116
void, free of duality 115

W

wake up 118, 129, 142, 144, 149, 155, 179, 184
warrior messiah 68, 176
Watts, Alan 116, 164, 165
wisdom sayings 65, 85
works 108
world problems 106
worship 82, 108

Z

zero-point field 125, 126

Index

Thank You!
We appreciate the time you took to read

The Gospel of Thomas: Where Science Meets Spirituality

A human being is part of the whole we call the Universe, a part limited in time and space. He experiences himself, his thoughts and feelings as something separated from the rest—a kind of optical illusion of his consciousness. This illusion is a prison for us, restricting us to our personal desires and affection for only the few people nearest us. Our task must be to free ourselves from this prison, by widening our circle of compassion, to embrace all living beings and all of nature.

—Albert Einstein

It is our heartfelt desire that you will allow nothing to stand in the way of your own experience of the Divine.

We invite you to join us at The Beginning of Fearlessness/Oroborus Books blog and website. We look forward to your comments:

www.thebeginningoffearlessness.com

www.ingramcontent.com/pod-product-compliance
Lightning Source LLC
Chambersburg PA
CBHW051649040426
42446CB00009B/1043